HOW TO
CROCHET

TECHNIQUES AND PROJECTS
FOR THE COMPLETE BEGINNER

EMMA VARNAM

THE GUILD OF MASTER CRAFTSMAN PUBLICATIONS

This updated edition published 2017 by
Guild of Master Craftsman Publications Ltd
Castle Place, 166 High Street, Lewes,
East Sussex, BN7 1XU, UK

First published 2014 by GMC Publications Ltd

Text © Emma Varnam, 2014
Copyright in the Work © GMC Publications Ltd, 2017

ISBN 978 1 78494 345 5

PUBLISHER Jonathan Bailey
PRODUCTION MANAGER Jim Bulley
SENIOR PROJECT EDITOR Wendy McAngus
EDITOR Nicola Hodgson
MANAGING ART EDITOR Gilda Pacitti
ART EDITOR Rebecca Mothersole
DESIGNER Luana Gobbo
ILLUSTRATORS Joshua Brent, Alexander Singleton and Martin Woodward
PHOTOGRAPHERS Sarah Cuttle and Rebecca Mothersole

Colour origination by GMC Reprographics
Printed and bound in Malaysia

For Daddy – thank you

CONTENTS

INTRODUCTION

A couple of years ago we inherited some vintage crochet blankets. Each blanket was countless colours, made from yarn recycled from old jumpers. Although the colour choices were random and often clashed, the whole piece looked fabulous. I felt compelled to make one myself, with the added incentive that I might at long last whittle down my ever-growing stash of yarn.

I set about teaching myself to crochet and was smitten immediately. Crochet seems to grow much faster than knitting, which makes creating a large garment or blanket far more appealing. With just one small hook required in the way of equipment, it is also easy to crochet on the go. As I gained more confidence I soon became enchanted with making small toys for my little boy. By working double-crochet stitches in a spiral you can create great three-dimensional shapes without any annoying seams – and that makes toys and accessories all the more durable.

I still really enjoy knitting, which I have done since childhood, but I now flip between the two crafts using the most appropriate technique for the project in hand. You will find that crochet is ideal for making household objects as well as great gifts.

In this book I have tried to introduce you to the essential techniques that will enable you to create some of the most useful and covetable patterns. Along the way I give you tips and hints that, I hope, will ensure you avoid the mistakes I made when I was a beginner.

If I have one piece of advice it is this: have fun with crochet. Try using lots of different colours and types of yarns. Many of the projects in this book are quick and easy and should ensure that you will be able to complete your projects fairly quickly. You will find that crochet is very satisfying and well worth sharing with friends.

BEFORE YOU START

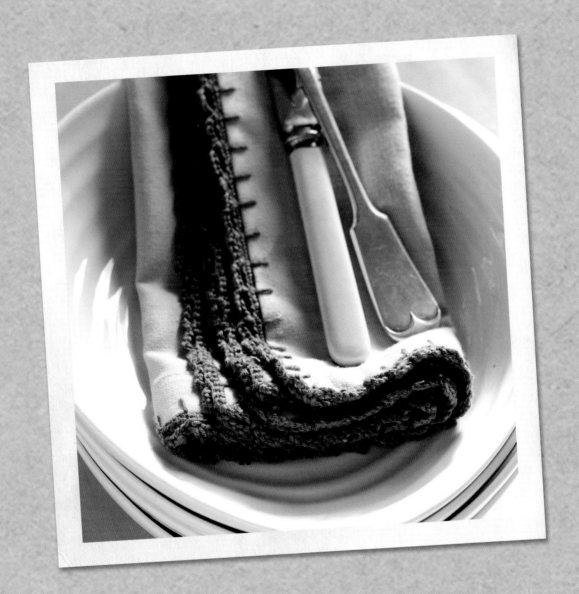

BASIC TOOLS AND EQUIPMENT

You don't need much equipment to start to crochet: with a crochet hook and a ball of yarn, you're ready to go. Many of the other pieces of equipment featured in this book are items you may already have at home. Experiment with a few stitches and the double-crochet pattern (see page 38) to see whether the craft is for you.

1 CROCHET HOOKS

Crochet hooks come in a range of sizes, which correspond to the weight (thickness) of the yarn. Very fine lace-weight yarns require a small hook, whereas if you are using chunky-weight yarn you will want a much thicker hook. The table on page 15 gives you an idea of which size hooks correspond to which yarn. The number on the hook is its diameter in millimetres and the sizing system is the same as that used for knitting needles. The ball band on a ball of yarn (the paper band) will carry a suggested size of hook for that yarn. Hooks come in materials including plastic, steel, aluminium, bamboo and wood. If you find you really enjoy crochet, then invest in a good-quality hook, as that will be easier to push through the stitches and helps you work faster and with a more even tension. The size of modern hooks is given in millimetres but older hooks are sized differently. The table on page 14 will help you identify your hooks.

2 SCISSORS

Have a small pair of scissors handy to cut the yarn when the project is finished. You can use any that you already have at home, but as you progress you may want a pair of sharp sewing scissors that will give a clean cut, making it easier to thread the yarn onto a tapestry needle to sew in the ends.

3 TAPE MEASURE

A small retractable tape measure is useful for measuring your work.

4 TAPESTRY NEEDLES

You will need a tapestry needle with a large eye to sew in the yarn ends, sew on buttons or complete any embroidery details to embellish a project.

5 PINS

Large-headed pins are useful to hold pieces of crochet fabric together while you are joining seams.

6 STITCH MARKERS

Markers are used to keep track of the beginning of a round when you work in the round (see page 58).

7 ROW COUNTER

Many crocheters find it useful to keep track of where they are in a pattern by using a row counter.

8 PLASTIC SAFETY EYES

To ensure a crochet toy is safe for children you should use safety eyes. These have a stem that is inserted through the crochet material and then secured with a washer.

9 STRAIGHT RULER

A ruler is ideal for measuring your crochet on a flat surface.

10 PENCIL AND NOTEBOOK

I like to use a notebook to keep track of where I am up to in a pattern. Sometimes I also use it to keep track of the number of rows I have completed or to make a note of where I might have altered the pattern.

Tip The ideal beginner's first hook is a 4mm (UK8:USG/6) metal hook used with a DK (double knit) yarn weight. These materials are easy to find and comfortable to work with while you are learning.

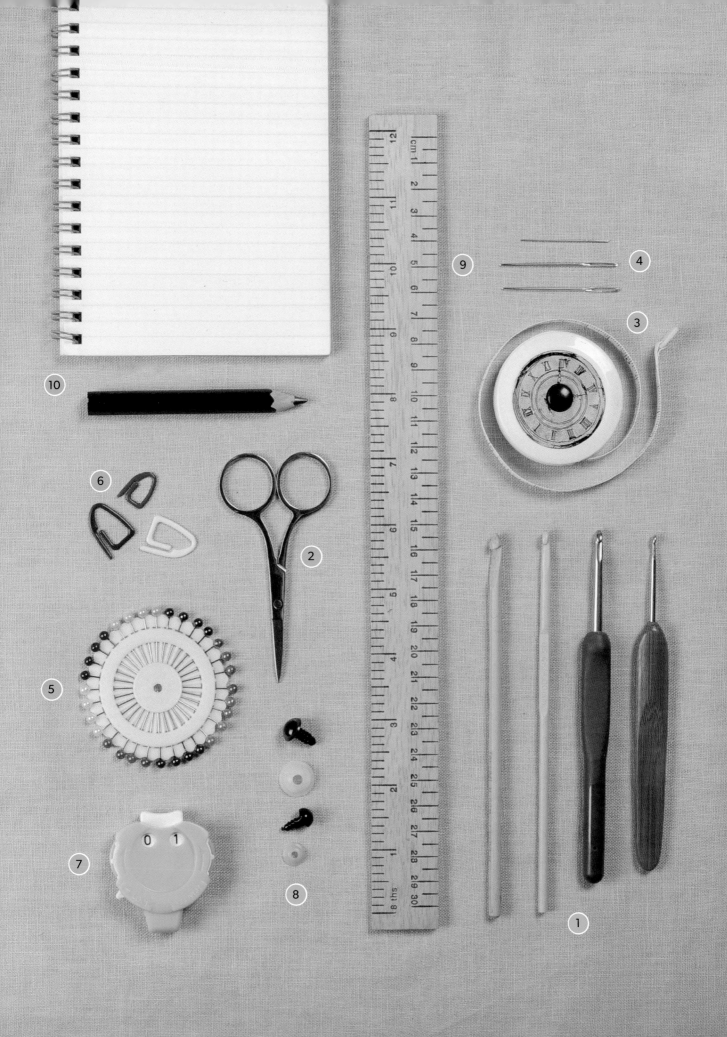

CROCHET-HOOK CONVERSIONS

UK	Metric	US		UK	Metric	US
14	2mm	–		7	4.5mm	7
13	2.25mm	B/1		6	5mm	H/8
12	2.5mm	–		5	5.5mm	I/9
–	2.75mm	C/2		4	6mm	J/10
11	3mm	–		3	6.5mm	K/10.5
10	3.25	D/3		2	7mm	–
9	3.5mm	E/4		0	8mm	L/11
–	3.75mm	F/5		00	9mm	M/N/13
8	4mm	G/6		000	10mm	N/P/15

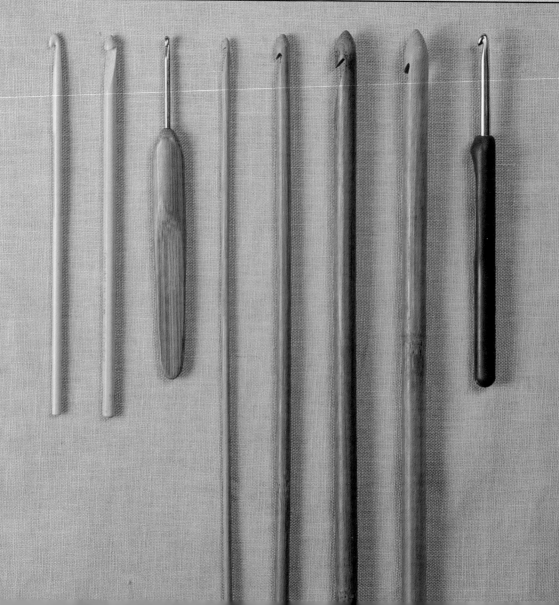

The chart below suggests hook sizes for
some of the commonly used yarn weights.

HOOK SIZE	UK YARN SIZE
2.5–3.5mm	4ply
3.5–4.5mm	DK
5–6mm	Aran
7mm and bigger	chunky

YARNS

In this book I have tried to use natural yarns that are easy to work with. All yarns are made up of thin strands of spun fibre. When they are twisted together they can make up yarn of varying thicknesses. My advice to any beginner crocheter is to use a yarn with a firm twist – one that doesn't unravel easily. This will be easy to work with and you know that your hook is going into the correct place in the crochet fabric.

There are many different yarn fibres available to buy and they all have different properties. Wool and cotton are probably the most commonly used fibres in crochet and are readily available. Wool is a warm, breathable, natural fibre taken from the fleece of sheep. Wool has an elasticity that is great for a beginner to work with and makes cosy garments. Cotton is a plant fibre and is available in different softnesses. Cotton is perfect for household or toy projects. It is strong, comes in a wide range of bright colours and can be washed at high temperatures without fading.

Yarns are sold in different thicknesses. Lace yarns or crochet threads are fine and use very thin crochet hooks. Thicker wool or cotton yarns go from 4ply through DK and Aran, up to chunky and super-chunky.

BUYING YARN FOR A CROCHET PATTERN

Choosing yarn is an important and pleasurable part of crochet. However, beginners are often tempted to buy a great-looking yarn that is not the type used in their chosen pattern and then don't understand why the finished article doesn't turn out like the photograph.

Always try to buy the yarn specified in your pattern. If you want to substitute a different yarn, you will need to find one that is the same weight (for example, DK or Aran) and one that works up to the same tension (see page 33). Check the meterage of your yarn (the total length of yarn to each ball – this information is printed on the ball band). There is nothing more frustrating than running out of yarn just before you reach the end of a project because your ball isn't as long as that used in the pattern.

CHECK THE BALL BAND

The ball band contains a wealth of information that is worth checking before you begin a project.

• Yarn weight and length – this tells you the length of the yarn on the ball as well as its weight (thickness).

• Hook/needle size – this suggests which size knitting needle or crochet hook to use (the sizing is the same).

• The standard tension to which the yarn is worked – this tells you the number of stitches and rows to each 4in (10cm) square.

• Yarn composition – the type and percentage of fibres in the yarn, for example 100% merino wool, or 50% wool, 50% cotton.

• Washing instructions – these are very important to ensure you don't spoil all your hard work in the wash.

• Shade number – this tells you the exact colour of the yarn as specified by the manufacturer.

• Dye lot – this is the number of the batch in which the yarn was dyed. If you need more than one ball for your project, always try to buy balls from the same dye lot as the colour can vary quite a bit from one batch to another. I have made some disastrous jumpers where you could clearly see a different band of colour due to an odd dye lot; it is an annoying and expensive mistake to make.

Tip When using different colours in your projects try not to mix different fibres, such as cotton and acrylic, within the same project. They will shrink at different rates during washing and this could distort the shape of your work.

BASIC TECHNIQUES

HOLDING THE HOOK

There are a number of ways that you can hold the hook.
Experiment to see which you find most comfortable.

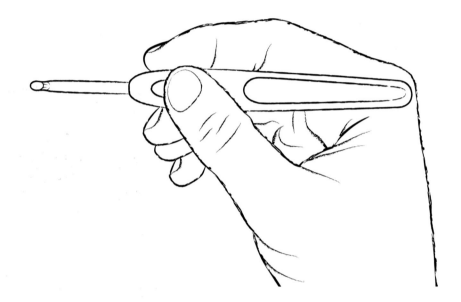

PENCIL METHOD

Hold the hook in either your right or left hand as you would a pen, in between your index finger and thumb, about 1¼–2in (3–5cm) from the hook end. If your hook has a flat handle then hold it there for comfort.

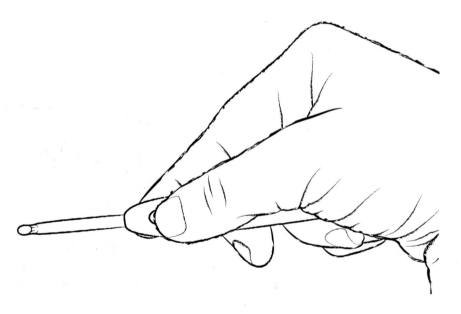

KNIFE METHOD

Hold your hook in either your right or left hand, between your thumb and forefinger, about 1¼–2in (3–5cm) from the hook and resting the handle against the palm of your hand.

HOLDING THE YARN

When you hold the yarn, the most important consideration is to create some tension between the yarn and the crochet hook. This will make it easier and quicker to wrap your yarn around the hook when making a stitch. Try both of the following methods to see which works best for you. Remember to keep your hands close together as you work.

You will find your finger inching along the stitches of the row as you work across. One of the hardest things beginners encounter is the feeling of crocheting in mid-air, with little control of the hook or the yarn. But if you follow these holding tips you will find it easier to work the stitches and your crochet will soon start looking neat and even.

FOREFINGER METHOD

Unwind a length of yarn from the ball. Wrap the end of the yarn around the little finger of the hand not holding the crochet hook, pass the yarn under your middle and ring fingers and then bring the yarn up and over your forefinger. Hold the chain or crochet fabric steady between the middle finger and thumb of the same hand. Raise your forefinger when you want to increase the tension in the yarn.

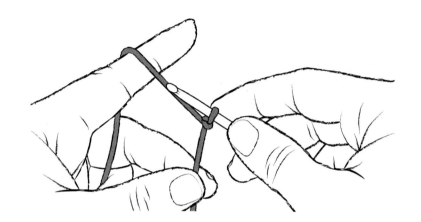

MIDDLE-FINGER METHOD

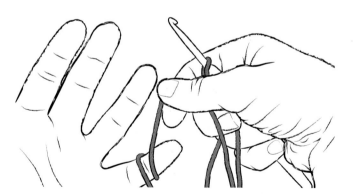

1 Unwind your yarn from the ball. Wrap the end of the yarn around the little finger of the hand not holding the crochet hook, then pass the yarn up between the little finger and the ring finger.

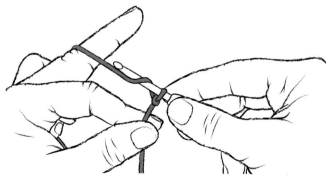

2 Pass the yarn over the back of your fingers. Hold the chain or crochet fabric steady between your forefinger and your thumb. Raise your middle finger when you want to increase the tension in the yarn.

MAKING A SLIP KNOT

Crochet starts by forming a slip knot, which is easy to tighten or loosen on your crochet hook.

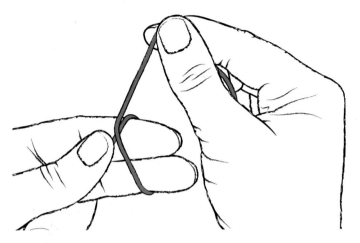

1 Make a loop of yarn over two fingers.

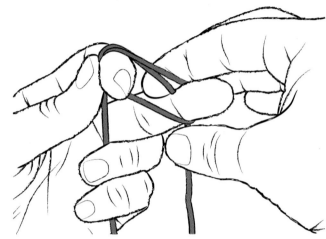

2 Pull a second loop through this first loop.

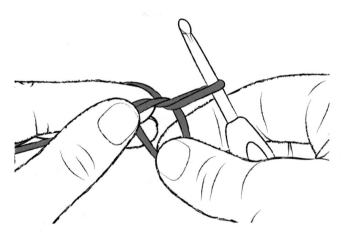

3 Pull up the loop and slip this loop onto your crochet hook.

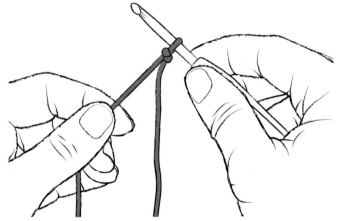

4 Pull both ends of the yarn to gently tighten the knot on the hook. You are now ready to make your first crochet stitch. (To undo a slip knot, remove the loop from the hook and pull both ends of the yarn.)

CHAIN STITCH (CH ST)

All crochet starts with chain. A length of chain forms the foundation row for crochet items that are worked in rows.

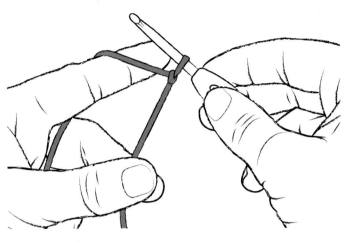

1 Make a slip knot on the hook.

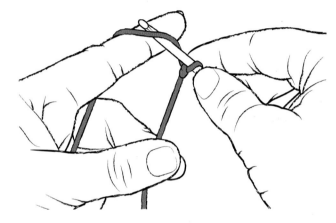

2 Wrap the yarn over the hook.

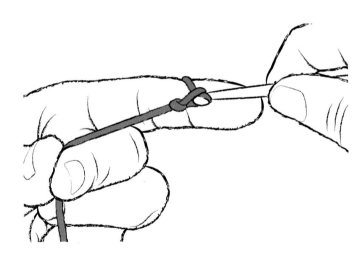

3 Pull the loop through the loop of the slip knot to form one chain stitch.

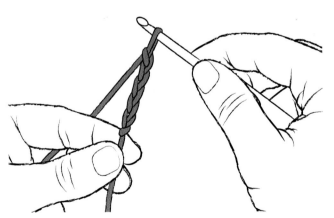

4 Repeat this process until you have the number of chain stitches required in your pattern instructions.

HOW TO COUNT CHAINS

When you are making chain stitches, each chain or loop counts as one stitch. Do not count the slip knot or the loop on the crochet hook when counting your chains.

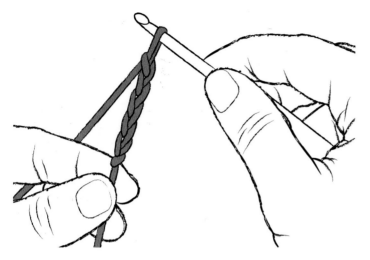

1 This drawing shows the right side of the chain. You can tell because you can spot the V-shaped stitches.

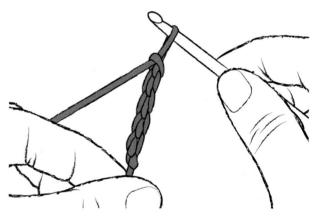

2 This is the back of the chain, which looks a bit more like a chain and does not have V-shaped stitches.

TURNING CHAINS

It is necessary to work a number of chain stitches at the beginning of each row or round to make an edge that is the height of the stitch you are about to make. This is called the turning chain. Making the right number of chain stitches to match your stitch will ensure that the sides of your work look straight (see the table, *right*). You also need to know which stitch of the previous row to place your first proper stitch into. For double crochet, the turning chain does not count as a stitch so the first stitch of a dc row is worked into the stitch at the base of the chain. For other stitches, however, the turning chains do count as the first stitch.

STITCH	TURNING CHAIN
Double crochet	1 ch
Half treble	2 ch
Treble	3 ch
Double treble	4 ch
Treble treble	5 ch

JOINING A RING

Circular pieces of crochet are started by making a length of chain
that is then joined into a ring.

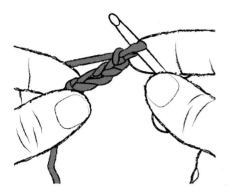

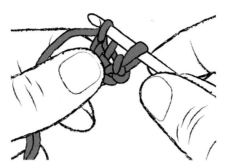

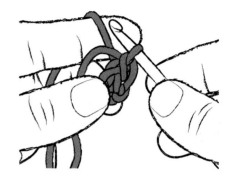

1 Work the number of chain stitches specified in the pattern instructions.

2 Insert the hook into the first chain stitch you made.

3 Wrap the yarn over the hook and pull through the two stitches on the hook to join the ring.

SLIP STITCH (SL ST)

This stitch is the most basic stitch. It has no height and is often used
to join rounds together. It is also useful for adding decoration and
for attaching two pieces of crochet together.

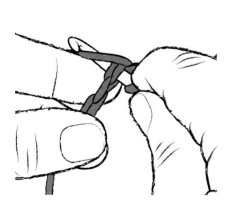

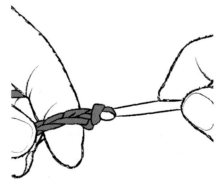

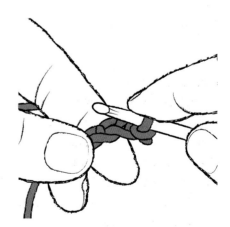

1 Insert the hook into a stitch. Wrap the yarn over the hook.

2 Draw the loop through the stitch and the loop on the hook.

3 Continue in this way to make the required number of slip stitches.

MAGIC CIRCLE

In recent years, with the increasing interest in making amigurumi or crochet toys, the magic-circle (also known as the magic-ring) technique has become popular. This is a neat way of starting a circular piece of crochet while avoiding the unsightly hole that can be left in the centre when you join a ring the normal way (see page 23). Magic circles are nearly always made with double-crochet stitches, as this creates a tight, dense crochet fabric suitable for toys and amigurumi objects.

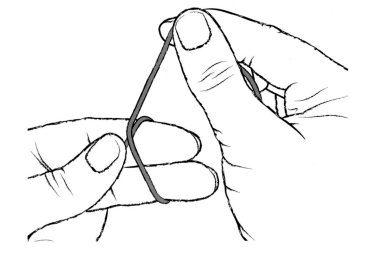

1 Start by making a basic slip knot. Make a loop of yarn over two fingers.

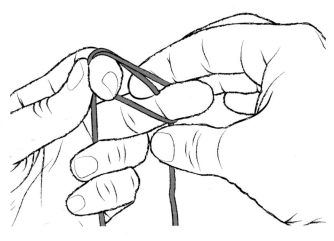

2 Pull a second loop through this first loop.

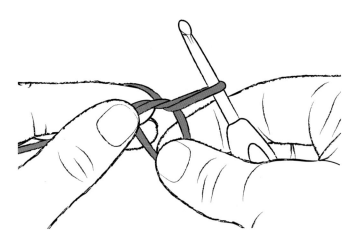

3 Pull up the loop and slip this loop onto your crochet hook.

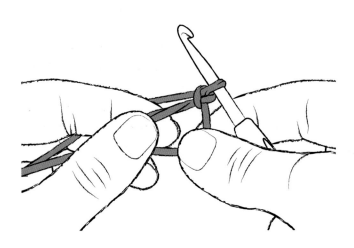

4 Before you tighten the ring, yarn over the hook (outside the circle) and pull through to make the first chain.

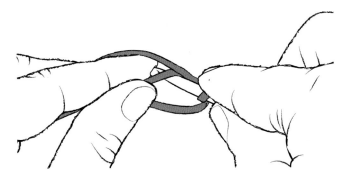

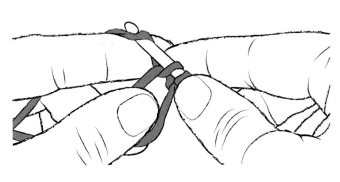

5 Insert the hook into the ring, yarn over the hook and pull through the ring so there are two loops on the hook.

6 Yarn over the hook again (outside the circle) and pull through both loops.

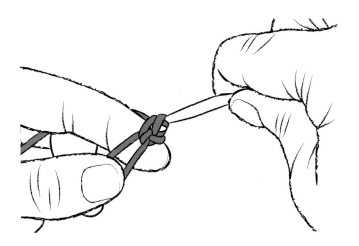

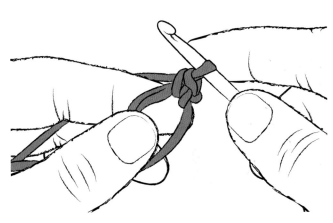

7 You have made your first double-crochet stitch.

8 Continue to work like this for as many double-crochet stitches as are stated in the pattern instructions.

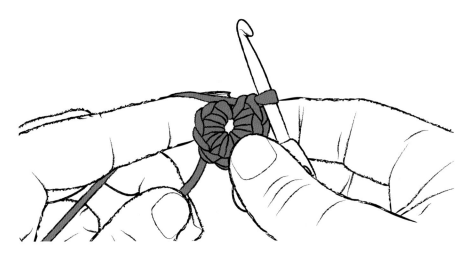

9 Pull the yarn tail to tighten the ring and then continue working in the round as usual.

Tip When you first attempt a magic circle it can seem really fiddly, but it is a technique worth practising because when you pull the tail of the yarn tightly you can almost make the centre hole disappear.

MAKING A HORIZONTAL BUTTONHOLE

Horizontal buttonholes are the easiest way to create buttonhole or thumbhole gaps in your crochet.

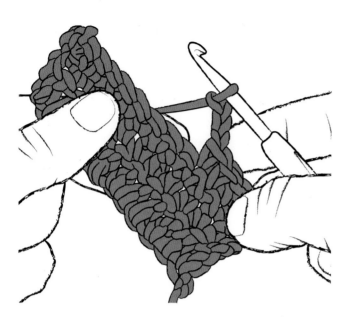

1 Work until you reach the place where you want the hole to be. Chain enough stitches to make a chain as long as the diameter of your button. Count how many stitches this was.

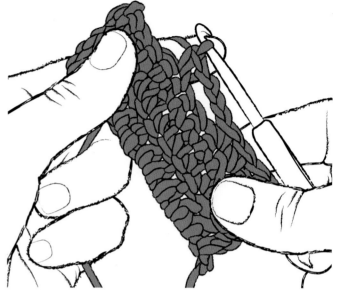

2 Skip the same number of stitches as were in the chain, and continue in your stitch pattern.

3 Continue in your stitch pattern to the end of your row. On the next row, work into the chain stitches as if you were working into the stitches as normal.

CHANGING COLOURS

Making sure that you change yarn colour neatly in the middle of your work can make a huge difference to the look of the final project. You can also use this technique to start a new ball of the same colour yarn if you have come to the end of your current ball in the middle of your work. This is the method to use if you are working in double crochet.

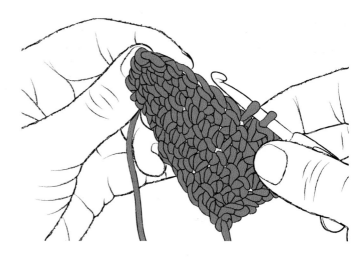

1 Crochet to the point where there are two loops of the last stitch before the colour change.

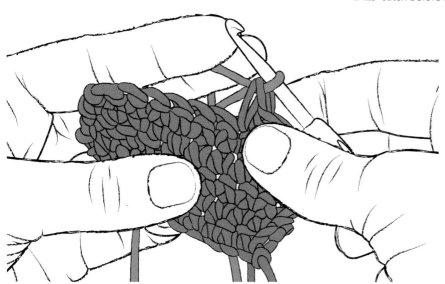

2 Drop the old colour, wrap the new colour of yarn over the hook and pull this new colour through both loops of the first colour.

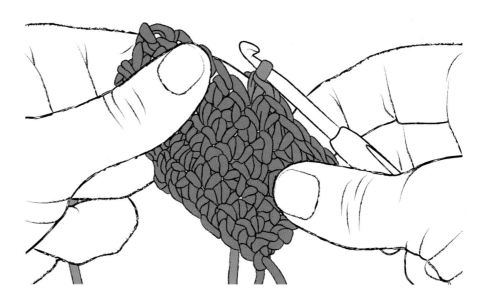

3 Using the second colour of yarn, you can now dc into the next stitch as usual.

MAKING A
CROCHETED CORD

You can make a very simple cord by making a length of chain stitches. However, this will not be very strong. An alternative is to make a crocheted cord, which is sturdier and also more decorative. Work a chain to the desired length, then work a slip stitch into each stitch of the chain to the end. If you want to make the cord even thicker, turn the work, make one chain (for the turning chain) and slip stitch down the chain one more time. Fasten off and weave in ends.

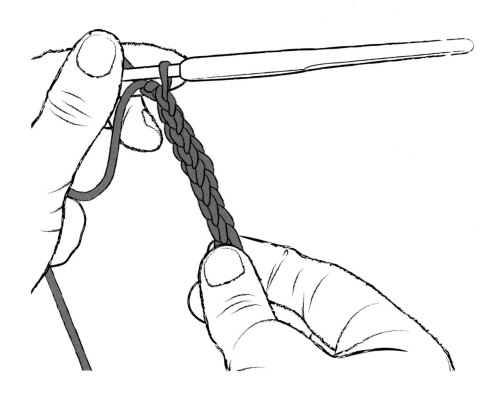

FASTENING OFF

After all your hard work you want to make sure that your finished piece will not unravel. Fastening your work off properly will ensure it is secure and gives a neat and professional-looking finish.

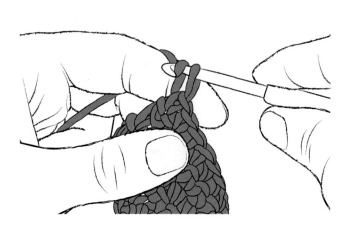

1 When you have finished your crochet, pull the last stitch through the loop on your hook.

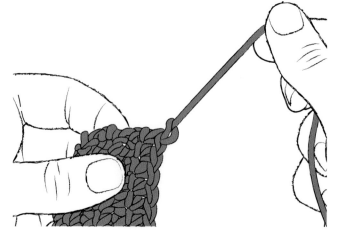

2 Cut the yarn leaving a 6in (15cm) tail, then thread this through the centre of the loop and pull tightly to form a small knot.

WEAVING IN ENDS

Making sure all your tails of yarn are woven in securely can make all the difference to the finished project.

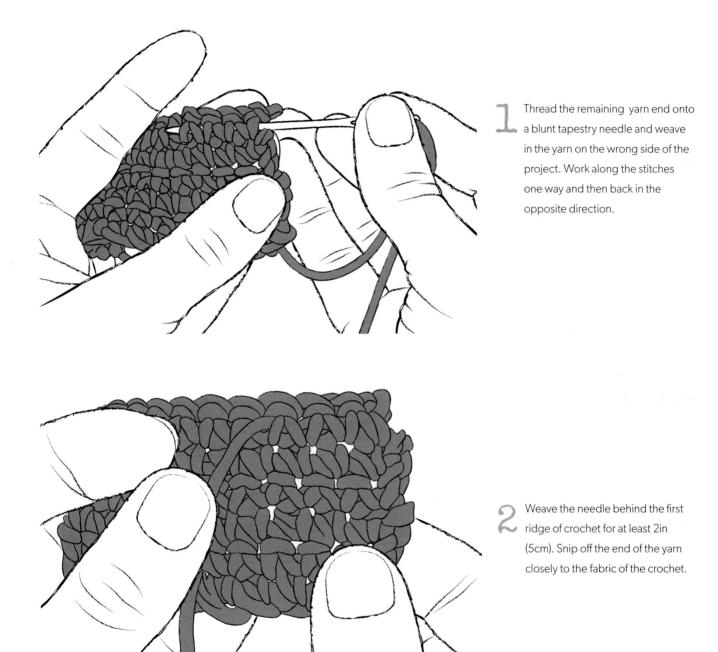

1 Thread the remaining yarn end onto a blunt tapestry needle and weave in the yarn on the wrong side of the project. Work along the stitches one way and then back in the opposite direction.

2 Weave the needle behind the first ridge of crochet for at least 2in (5cm). Snip off the end of the yarn closely to the fabric of the crochet.

Tip When you start a new ball of yarn, leave a tail of at least 6in (15cm) instead of a fiddly short tail that would be difficult to thread through a needle when it comes to weaving in the ends.

FOLLOWING PATTERNS

When people first see crochet patterns, they often get scared because the instructions appear to be written in code. Don't worry – they are actually just abbreviations (see opposite). You will soon remember what they stand for and will become fully fluent in the language of crochet.

At the beginning of the pattern there will be a summary of the materials you will need, including the type and quantity of yarn required and the recommended size of hook.

Make sure you have all your equipment gathered together before you start work. This will ensure you are more likely to finish the project, rather than running out of yarn and coming to a standstill.

The pattern will also include a summary of the stitches and techniques used. This will help you work out how difficult you might find this pattern. If there is a stitch or technique you have never used before, try it out on a sample swatch before you start.

ASTERISKS

When the asterisk symbol * appears in a pattern this means you need to repeat a stitch or a section. The pattern will explain which part to repeat. You must repeat this pattern sequence precisely to ensure the pattern works properly.

BRACKETS

Instructions enclosed in brackets must be worked in the order given and repeated using the instructions following the brackets. For example: (2 dc, dc2tog) 4 times. The details in brackets are a detail of the pattern that must be repeated four times in this case.

STITCH COUNT

Often a stitch count is provided at the end of each row or round. This tells you how many stitches should be in that row and is a useful way of checking that your work is on track.

HOW TO COUNT STITCHES

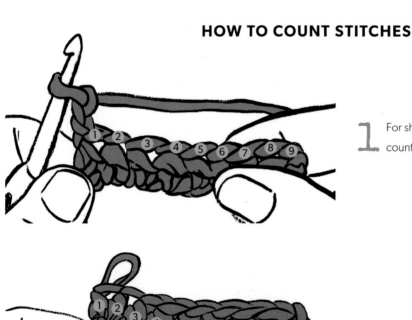

1 For short-stitch patterns such as double crochet, count the V-shaped tops of the stitches.

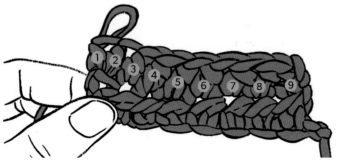

2 For longer stitches such as treble crochet, count the upright stems.

UK AND US DIFFERENCES

UK and US crochet terms have different meanings, which can cause confusion. This book is written using UK terms. When you go on to work from different patterns, you will need to check whether the pattern is written with UK or US terms. Checking this detail will ensure your crochet develops correctly – there is nothing more frustrating than working on a pattern and then realizing it is completely wrong and needs to be unravelled.

UK crochet terms	US crochet terms
Double crochet	Single crochet
Half treble	Half double crochet
Treble	Double crochet
Double treble	Triple crochet
Treble treble	Double triple crochet

ABBREVIATIONS

blo	back loop only	m	metre(s)
ch	chain	mm	millimetre(s)
ch sp	chain space	rep	repeat
cm	centimetre(s)	RS	right side
dc	double crochet	sl st	slip stitch
dc2tog	double crochet two stitches together (decrease by one stitch)	sp	space
DK	double knitting	st(s)	stitch(es)
dtr	double treble	tog	together
g	gram(s)	tr	treble
htr	half treble	tr2tog	treble two stitches together (decrease by one stitch)
htr2tog	half treble two stitches together (decrease by one stitch)	trtr	treble treble
		WS	wrong side
in	inch(es)	yd	yard(s)

READING CHARTS

Some crocheters find it easier to work from pattern charts that are made with symbols rather than reading the pattern in words. Crochet symbols are universal, and the same symbols are used to refer to the same stitch around the globe.

Once you have understood what each symbol means, there are a number of rules that make it easier to read charts.

Charts that are worked in rows start from the bottom and are worked upwards in the direction you are crocheting. Once you have completed the chain foundation, you work right to left, turn your work, and then work from the chart left to right.

Charts that are worked in rounds start in the centre. You read the chart working from the centre to the outside and in an anticlockwise direction.

The beginning place is often marked with a small arrow. If the beginning is not marked, look for the first row or for the middle of the round.

Charts do not distinguish whether you should crochet into the stitch or into a loop made by the stitch. Therefore it is worth double checking in the written pattern to be sure where you should place your stitch.

HOW TO READ THE SYMBOLS

Symbol		Symbol		Symbol	
▶	Start of pattern	⬭	Chain	⊤	Treble crochet
◯	Magic circle	+	Double crochet	⊥	Double treble crochet
●	Slip stitch	⊤	Half treble crochet	⤬⤬	2 dc into next st

THE IMPORTANCE OF TENSION

Tension is one of the most important factors in creating a successful project. If you don't achieve the correct number of stitches and rows to match the tension quoted in the pattern, then you won't have the correct measurements when your work is completed and the project will not turn out as it should.

First, make a tension swatch of about 6in (15cm) square using the hook and the stitch quoted in the pattern. This will enable you to measure accurately against the tension gauge quoted, which usually gives the number of stitches and rows over 4in (10cm) square. It is worth knowing that stitches at the end and beginning of rows are always tighter than the main body of the fabric, so making a larger swatch enables you to obtain a more accurate reading by measuring in the centre of the square.

Once you have finished your swatch, lay it out flat on a hard surface and leave the yarn square to relax for about an hour. Then, taking a rigid flat ruler, measure out the 4in (10cm) square tension area in the centre of the swatch. Mark the beginning and end of this section with pins and count the number of stitches between the pins. Do the same for the rows.

If you discover you have more stitches or rows between the pins than suggested, you are working to a tighter tension than recommended. Try again, using a larger hook.

If you have fewer stitches or rows than suggested, then you are working to a looser tension than recommended. Try again, using a smaller hook.

FINISHING

One of the biggest concerns that new crocheters face is that their finished work doesn't look quite like the sample photograph in the book or magazine they are following. How your work is finished will make a huge difference to the end result.

BLOCKING AND PRESSING YOUR WORK

One of the most useful techniques is learning to 'block' your work into shape once it is finished. Blocking your work can really transform your projects. During the making process the fibres of the yarn can often become crumpled and creased. By blocking your work, the fibres can relax, and the stitches become regular.

There are a number of techniques that can be used, so choose the most appropriate one for your project. Toys, amigurumi items, bags and coasters do not usually need to be blocked. Items such as lacy shawls, scarves and blankets should be hard blocked. Garments can either be wet blocked or steam blocked. In all cases, the items need to be wet enough that the fibres relax and you can reshape them into their final position. In all cases of blocking, make sure you leave the crochet to dry completely. Ideally you should leave your work for two or three days if you can.

BLOCKING REQUIREMENTS

First, check the ball band to ensure that the yarn will withstand getting wet, and make sure you have some rustproof pins. You will need space to lay out your blocked project to dry. Many people use a piece of hardboard covered with towels. Smaller projects can be blocked on an ironing board.

HARD BLOCKING

Lay your project on your blocking surface. Start at one corner and pin gradually along the edges, gently pulling the crochet into place, and secure with a pin. As you work around the edges, you might notice that you have pulled one area more taut than another. Simply remove the pins and reshape. Once you are happy with the overall dimensions, spray the item all over with tepid water. Leave to dry.

WET BLOCKING

Soak the item in lukewarm water. Add a little no-rinse wool wash and leave for around 20 minutes. Drain your sink and very gently squeeze out the water, but do not wring the crochet. Ensure that you scoop your item out of the sink; do not hang it out as this will stretch the fibres. Lay the item between two towels and gently roll up to remove as much of the excess water as possible. You can then lay your item out on your blocking surface and gently pin it out to the measurements you require. Leave to dry.

STEAM BLOCKING

This is a slightly faster version of wet blocking and is good for removing persistent creases from garments. Lay your crochet out on the blocking surface and use a steam iron or garment steamer to allow the hot steam to permeate the fibres. Make sure you don't let the iron touch the crochet because it will flatten textured stitches and totally ruin any acrylic yarn, making the crochet limp and lifeless.

Tip Children's foam play mats linked together can form a very large blocking area, ideal for blankets.

SEAMING

Once you have spent some time working on your crochet project you really want it to be robust and hard-wearing. This means that your finishing should be sturdy. You can use different seaming techniques for different projects.

1 WHIP STITCH

Use whip stitch if you want to sew your seams together. Place the two pieces of crochet wrong sides together and push a tapestry needle threaded with yarn through the stitches at the edge of both pieces. Repeat evenly along the edge so there is a row of small stitches. Whip stitch is very useful when you are attaching limbs and body parts when making toys. Use small, neat stitches to attach one part to another. Try not to flatten limbs as you sew, so that they will retain their rounded shape.

2 SLIP-STITCH SEAM

I often use a slip-stitch seam as it is a neat and strong way of attaching crochet pieces together. Place the crochet pieces together. Insert the hook through both edge stitches, yarn over hook, pull up a loop and chain one stitch. Work a row of slip stitches by inserting your hook through both sides at the same time. Keep the work fairly loose.

3 DOUBLE-CROCHET SEAM

A double-crochet seam is useful for joining two straight edges together. It can be worked on the right side of the work and used as a decorative edge. Place two pieces of crochet together, either with the right sides or wrong sides together. Insert the hook through both edge stitches, yarn over hook, pull up a loop and then work one double-crochet stitch. Then work in double crochet as usual along the edge. If you work around a corner, work three dc stitches into the corner stitch.

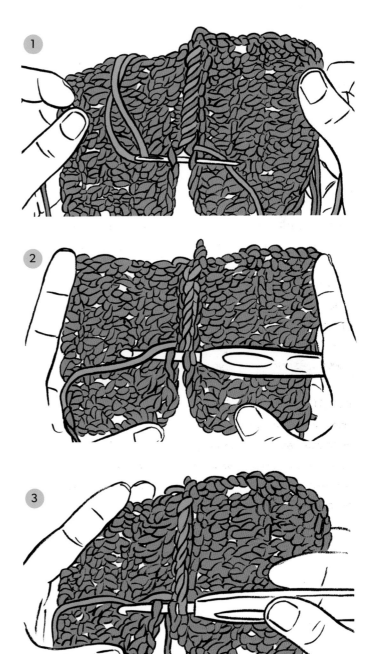

Tip If you leave a long yarn end when fastening off each piece you can use this for sewing the parts together.

TECHNIQUES
& PROJECTS

DOUBLE CROCHET

DOUBLE CROCHET IS THE SHORTEST AND MOST BASIC STITCH THAT IS USED TO MAKE CROCHET FABRIC. ONCE YOU HAVE MASTERED THIS LOVELY DENSE STITCH, YOU WILL BE ALL SET TO START MAKING A WIDE RANGE OF BEAUTIFUL CROCHET PROJECTS.

Double crochet is a short stitch that makes a dense fabric perfect for creating toys, accessories and homeware items that might be subjected to a bit of wear and tear.

My advice to the novice crocheter would be to begin by making a simple double-crochet cover for something, such as the tablet cover on page 42.

During the process you will get used to holding the hook and making loops. You'll find holding the yarn will come to feel less fiddly, and you will soon end up with a useful new accessory.

Tip Double-crochet rows look the same on both the front and the back of the work.

HOW TO GET STRAIGHT EDGES

Many beginners find it frustrating that their crochet does not end up with straight edges – they seem to magically add stitches without understanding why or how. To avoid this happening, you need to make the right number of turning chains at the beginning of each row (see page 22). This forms the edge for you to make your new row next to.

For double crochet you need to make just one turning chain (see below) but for taller stitches you will need more.

To get straight edges you also need to place your first proper stitch into the correct stitch of the previous row. For double crochet, the first stitch of a row is always worked into the stitch at the base of the turning chain.

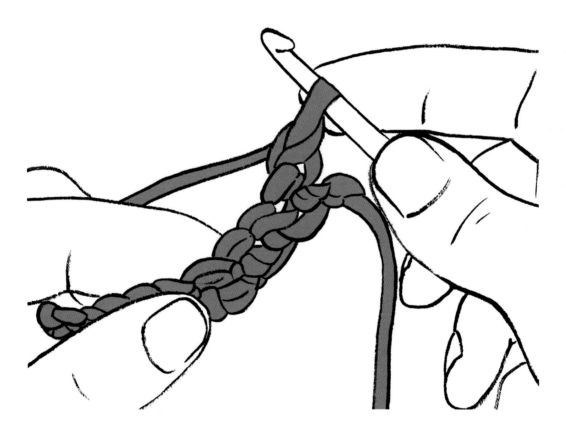

Tip Note that for double crochet the turning chain does not count as a stitch. With the longer crochet stitches, including treble-crochet stitches, the turning chain does count as a stitch.

MAKING DOUBLE CROCHET (DC)

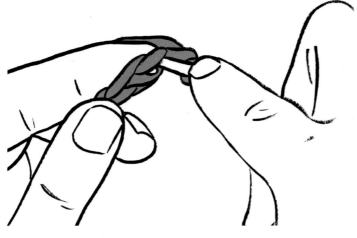

1 Make a chain to the length required in the pattern you are following. With the right side of the chain facing you (see page 22) locate the second chain from the hook.

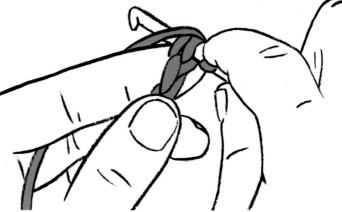

2 Insert the hook through the centre of this chain stitch. Push the hook underneath and then around the yarn. This is called yarn over hook.

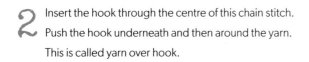

3 Catch the yarn with your hook and pull it through the chain stitch only. This means that you will now have two loops on your hook.

4 Yarn over hook (push the hook underneath and then around the yarn).

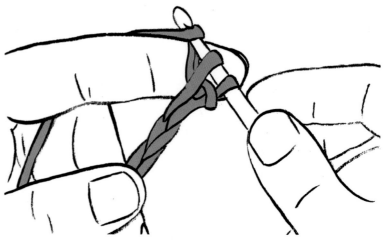

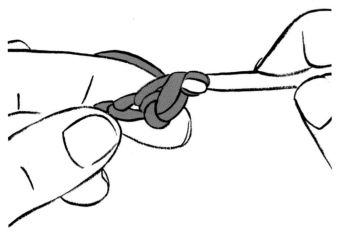

5   Pull yarn through both the loops on the hook, leaving one loop on the hook. This is the first double-crochet stitch.

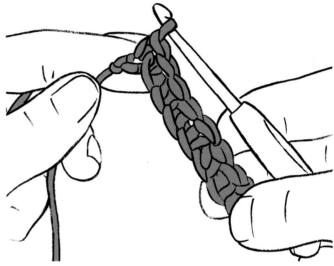

6   Continue to work one double-crochet stitch into each chain stitch (steps 2 to 5) until your first row of double-crochet stitches is complete. Note that the total number of stitches will be one fewer than the chain-stitch count.

7   Turn the work so that the crochet you have just made is in your free hand and the reverse side is facing you. Then chain one stitch. This is the turning chain (see page 22).

8   Work a second row of double crochet by inserting the hook under the top two threads of the first row of double-crochet stitches (these strands will look like a V-shape). Turn your work and repeat until your piece is the size required.

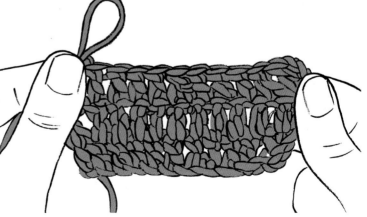

Project one

TABLET COVER

THIS IS A PERFECT BEGINNERS' PROJECT. THE TYPE OF YARN AND THE SIZE OF HOOK MEAN THE COVER GROWS QUICKLY AND THE PROJECT HELPS YOU PRACTISE KEEPING YOUR EDGES STRAIGHT. DOUBLE CROCHET CREATES A ROBUST FABRIC THAT WILL PROTECT YOUR GADGET PERFECTLY.

YOU WILL NEED

- Rowan All Seasons Cotton, 60% cotton, 40% acrylic (98yd/90m per 50g ball): 1 x 50g ball in 235 Tornado
- 4mm (UK8:USG/6) crochet hook
- 1 x 1in (2.5cm) button
- Tapestry needle

TENSION

15.5 sts and 8 rows to 4in (10cm) over double crochet using 4mm hook. Use a larger or smaller hook if necessary to obtain the correct tension.

FINISHED SIZE

10¼in x 7½in (26 x 19cm)

TECHNIQUES USED

Double crochet (see page 38)
Slip stitch (see page 23)

INSTRUCTIONS

COVER

Row 1: Using 4mm hook, ch 36 sts.
Row 2 (WS): 1 dc in 2nd ch from hook, dc into each ch to end, turn (35 sts).
Row 3: Ch 1, dc into each stitch to end.
Row 3 forms the pattern. Work a further 67 rows.
Fasten off and weave in ends.

BUTTONHOLE LOOP

With WS facing, join yarn to the 18th stitch, ch 40, sl st back into the same st to create the buttonhole loop. Fasten off and weave in ends.

FINISHING

With RS together, slip stitch or oversew both sides of the cover together. Fasten off and weave in the ends. Sew a button on the front of the cover to correspond to the end of the buttonhole loop. Put the button through the loop to keep the tablet safely in its cover.

Tip At the end of the day you can ensure that your work doesn't unravel by removing the hook and attaching a safety pin in the last loop and carefully pinning it to your crochet fabric.

TREBLE CROCHET

TREBLE CROCHET IS PERHAPS THE MOST COMMONLY USED AND VERSATILE STITCH IN CROCHET.
IT HAS MORE HEIGHT THAN DOUBLE CROCHET AND ALSO CREATES A MORE OPEN FABRIC.
WHEN COMBINED WITH OTHER STITCHES, IT CAN FORM LOTS OF INTERESTING PATTERNS.

Like double crochet, when worked in rows, treble crochet has the advantage of looking the same on both sides of the fabric. In the cushion cover project (see page 48), the treble crochet stitch is worked in rows, but you will also see this stitch worked in the round and it is the stitch most frequently used to make a crochet square.

MAKING TREBLE CROCHET (TR)

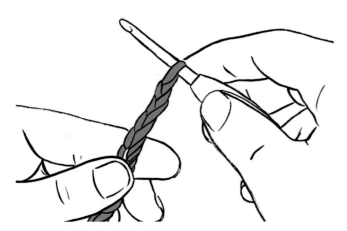

1 Work the number of chain stitches required for your foundation chain.

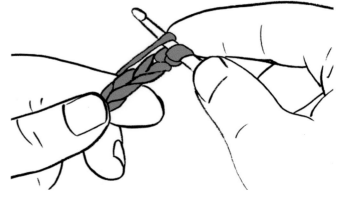

2 Yarn over hook.

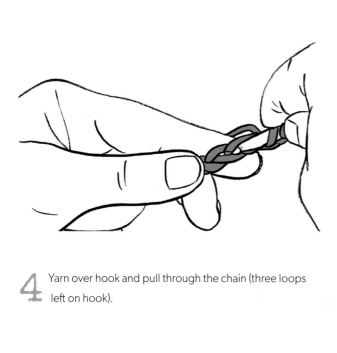

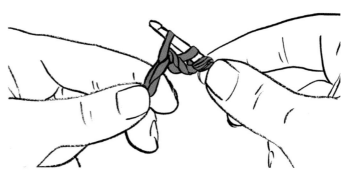

3 Insert your hook in the fourth chain from the hook (the first three chains of the foundation chain count as the first treble crochet stitch).

4 Yarn over hook and pull through the chain (three loops left on hook).

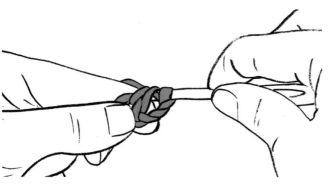

5 Yarn over hook.

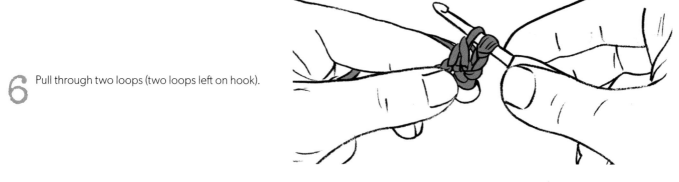

6 Pull through two loops (two loops left on hook).

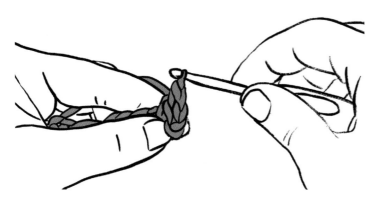

7 Yarn over hook and pull through the remaining two loops (one loop left on hook). Continue to work like this, making a treble crochet stitch in each chain to complete your first row. The total number of stitches will be three less than the original chain-stitch count.

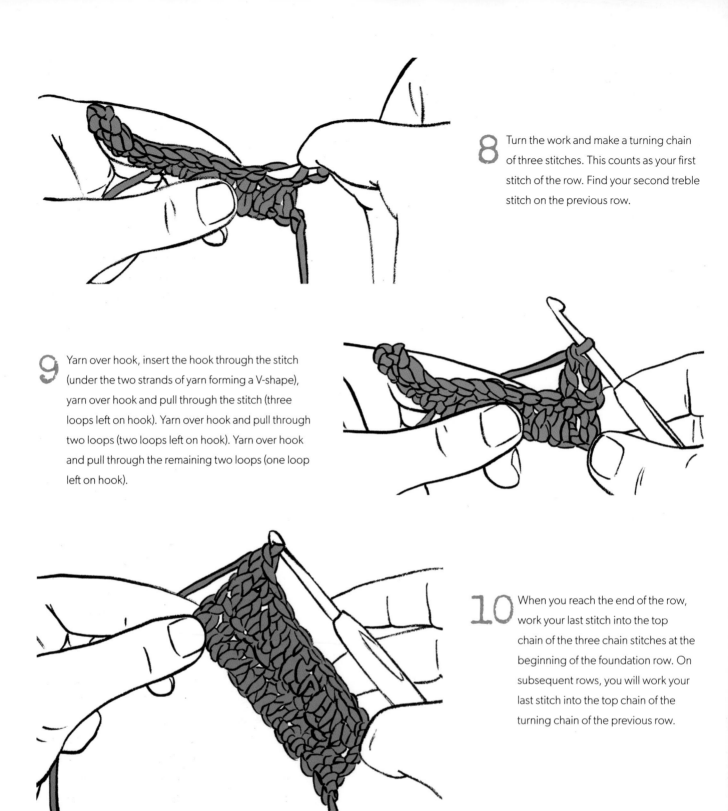

8 Turn the work and make a turning chain of three stitches. This counts as your first stitch of the row. Find your second treble stitch on the previous row.

9 Yarn over hook, insert the hook through the stitch (under the two strands of yarn forming a V-shape), yarn over hook and pull through the stitch (three loops left on hook). Yarn over hook and pull through two loops (two loops left on hook). Yarn over hook and pull through the remaining two loops (one loop left on hook).

10 When you reach the end of the row, work your last stitch into the top chain of the three chain stitches at the beginning of the foundation row. On subsequent rows, you will work your last stitch into the top chain of the turning chain of the previous row.

Tip Even the most experienced crocheter has to double-check that they have not missed any stitches or added a few stitches by mistake. After every few rows, stop to count your stitches to make sure everything is going to plan.

MAKING HALF TREBLE CROCHET (HTR)

The half treble crochet stitch comes between double crochet and
treble crochet in terms of height. It is taller than double crochet,
and requires two chain stitches for the turning chain (see page 22).

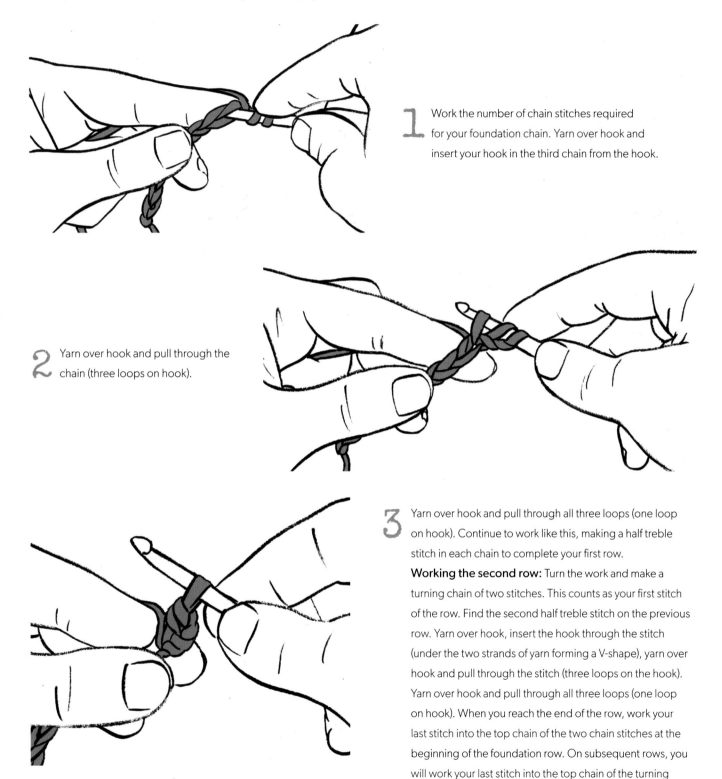

1 Work the number of chain stitches required
for your foundation chain. Yarn over hook and
insert your hook in the third chain from the hook.

2 Yarn over hook and pull through the
chain (three loops on hook).

3 Yarn over hook and pull through all three loops (one loop
on hook). Continue to work like this, making a half treble
stitch in each chain to complete your first row.

Working the second row: Turn the work and make a
turning chain of two stitches. This counts as your first stitch
of the row. Find the second half treble stitch on the previous
row. Yarn over hook, insert the hook through the stitch
(under the two strands of yarn forming a V-shape), yarn over
hook and pull through the stitch (three loops on the hook).
Yarn over hook and pull through all three loops (one loop
on hook). When you reach the end of the row, work your
last stitch into the top chain of the two chain stitches at the
beginning of the foundation row. On subsequent rows, you
will work your last stitch into the top chain of the turning
chain of the previous row.

CUSHION COVER

IF YOU ARE NEW TO CROCHET, THIS IS A GREAT PROJECT TO PRACTISE YOUR TREBLE CROCHET STITCH, MAKING SURE YOUR EDGES ARE STRAIGHT AND DEVELOPING EVEN STITCHES. PICK YOUR FAVOURITE COLOUR FOR THE CUSHION AND USE A CONTRASTING COLOUR AT THE EDGES.

YOU WILL NEED

- Rowan All Seasons Cotton, 60% cotton, 40% acrylic (98yd/90m per 50g ball): 6 x 50g balls in 241 Damson (A) 1 x 50g ball in 252 Atlas (B)
- 4mm (UK8:USG/6) crochet hook
- 2 x 1in (2.5cm) buttons
- Tapestry needle

TENSION

12.5 sts and 8 rows to 4in (10cm) over treble crochet using 4mm hook.
Use a larger or smaller hook if necessary to obtain the correct tension.

FINISHED SIZE

15¾in (40cm) square

TECHNIQUES USED

Double crochet (dc) (see page 38)
Treble crochet (tr) (see page 44)
Slip stitch (sl st) (see page 23)
Making buttonholes (see page 26)

INSTRUCTIONS

COVER

Row 1: Using 4mm hook and B, ch 61 sts.
Row 2 (WS): 1 dc in 2nd ch from hook, dc into each ch to end, turn (60 sts).
Row 3: Ch 1 (does not count as a st), dc in each st to end, turn (60 sts).
Row 4: Change to A, ch 3 (counts as first tr), miss st at the base of the ch, *1 tr in next st; rep from * to end, turn (60 sts).
Row 4 forms the pattern. Continue until work measures 35in (90cm).
Next row: Ch 1, dc in each st to end, turn (60 sts).
Work 3 more rows in dc.
Next row (buttonhole row): Ch 1, 18 dc, 3 ch, miss 3 dc, 18 dc, 3 ch, miss 3 dc, 18 dc, turn (60 sts).
Work 2 more rows in dc.
Next row: Change to B, ch 1, dc in each st to end, turn (60 sts).
Work 1 more row in dc.
Fasten off and weave in ends.

FINISHING

Lay the cushion out in front of you widthways with RS facing. Fold the buttonhole edge across and lay it on top of the crochet so that the buttonholes are 8in (20cm) from the edge. Then fold the starting edge across on top so that it overlaps the buttonholes. Make sure your cushion is square; it should measure 15¾in (40cm) wide and 15¾in (40cm) high. Slip stitch both sides of the cover together. Fasten off and weave in ends. Turn the cushion cover RS out. Sew buttons on the cover to correspond to the buttonholes.

INCREASING AND DECREASING

ONE OF THE BEST THINGS ABOUT CROCHET IS BEING ABLE TO CREATE A SCULPTURAL SHAPE SIMPLY BY INCREASING AND DECREASING THE NUMBER OF STITCHES. SO IF YOU MASTER THESE STRAIGHTFORWARD TECHNIQUES YOU'LL SOON SEE YOUR WORK TAKING SHAPE.

In the patterns and examples in this book, you will use various simple methods to increase and decease your stitches by a small number. Increases and decreases can be made anywhere on the row or the round.

Increases add fullness to the work. The easiest way to make an increase is to work two stitches into the same stitch (to increase by one stitch).

To decrease by one stitch you need to make two incomplete stitches, then you finish the decrease by working these two incomplete stitches together. Another simple way of decreasing is simply to miss stitches. This technique works best at the end of rows.

As you progress with your crochet you will come across more methods of increasing and decreasing with more stitches at a time.

Tip When making toys you can make an invisible double-crochet decrease by working just into the front loops of the two stitches you are working together.

INCREASING IN THE MIDDLE OF A ROW OR ROUND

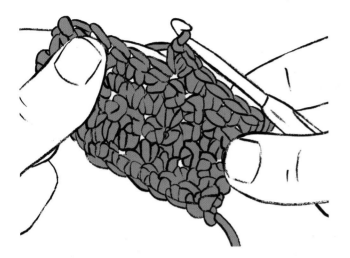

To increase by one stitch, work one stitch as normal, then insert the hook into the same stitch of the previous row and complete another stitch. Work to the end of your row or round. If you work into the same stitch three times, you will increase your stitch count by two.

INCREASING ONE STITCH AT EACH END OF A ROW

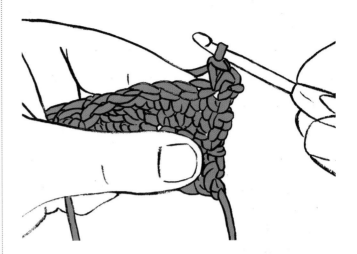

Work your normal turning chain, then work two stitches into the first stitch of your row. Work to the end of the row. Work two stitches into the very last stitch of your row.

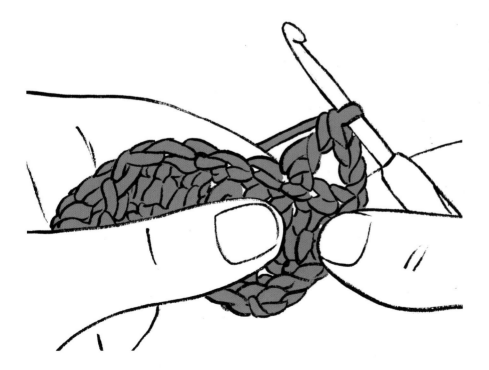

DECREASING ONE STITCH AT EACH END OF A ROW

Work your normal turning chain, then miss the first stitch of your row; work your next stitch in the second stitch. Work until you have two stitches left on the previous row. Miss one stitch and work into the last stitch for double crochet or into the turning chain for any of the longer stitches.

DECREASING ONE STITCH IN DOUBLE CROCHET (DC2TOG) IN THE MIDDLE OF A ROW OR ROUND

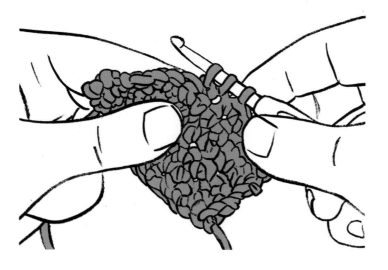

1 Insert your hook into the next stitch, pull a loop through (first incomplete stitch; two loops on hook). Insert your hook into the next stitch, pull a loop through (second incomplete stitch; three loops on hook).

2 Yarn over hook and pull the yarn through all three loops (decrease completed; one loop left on hook). One stitch decreased.

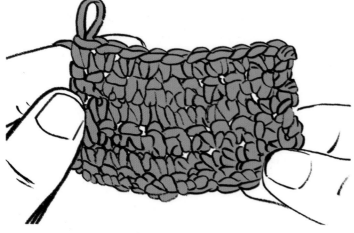

3 Continue to work in double crochet to the end of the row. You will have decreased the row by one stitch.

Tip Most crochet patterns will give you a stitch count at the end of any row which has increases or decreases – take time to make sure you have the right number of stitches in each row.

DECREASING ONE STITCH IN TREBLE CROCHET (TR2TOG)
IN THE MIDDLE OF A ROW OR ROUND

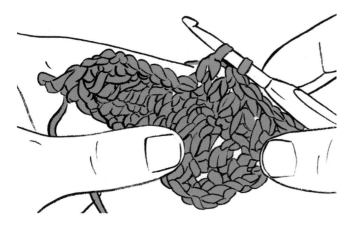

1 Yarn over hook, insert the hook through the stitch, yarn over hook and pull through the stitch (three loops on hook). Yarn over hook and pull through two loops (first incomplete stitch; two loops on hook).

2 Yarn over hook, insert your hook into the next stitch, pull a loop through, yarn over hook and pull through the first two loops on the hook (second incomplete stitch; three loops on hook).

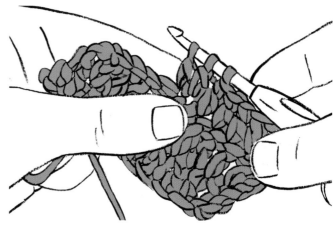

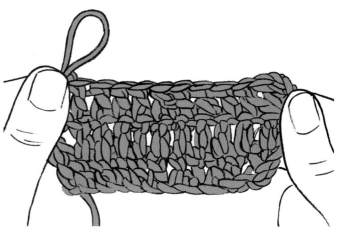

3 Yarn over hook and then pull the yarn through all three loops (decrease completed; one loop left on hook). One stitch decreased.

4 Continue to work in treble crochet to the end of the row. You will have decreased the row by one stitch.

RASPBERRY TEA COSY

THIS COSY IS WORKED IN HALF TREBLE STITCH AND USES BOTH THE DECREASE TECHNIQUES OF MISSING STITCHES AND OF WORKING TWO STITCHES TOGETHER. THE CROCHETED-CORD LOOP FORMS A DECORATIVE LEAF AT THE TOP AND ALSO WORKS AS A PRACTICAL HANGING LOOP.

YOU WILL NEED

- Woolyknit Crafts Aran, 100% wool (85yd/77m per 50g ball):
  2 x 50g balls in 022 Redberry (A)
  1 x 50g ball in 020 Apple (B)
- 4mm (UK8:USG/6) crochet hook
- 2 x ¾in (2cm) buttons
- Tapestry needle

TENSION

17 sts and 14 rows to 4in (10cm) over half treble crochet using 4mm hook. Use a larger or smaller hook if necessary to obtain the correct tension.

FINISHED SIZE

7½in (19cm) wide and 6in (15cm) high to fit a standard six-cup teapot

TECHNIQUES USED

Half treble crochet (htr) (see page 47)
Double crochet (dc) (see page 38)
Slip stitch (sl st) (see page 23)
Increasing (see page 51)
Decreasing (see page 52)
Making a crocheted cord (see page 28)

TECHNIQUE NOTE

To make a half treble decrease (htr2tog): Yarn over hook, insert hook through stitch, yarn over hook and pull yarn through stitch (three loops on hook).

Yarn over hook, insert hook into next stitch, pull yarn through stitch, yarn over hook and pull through all five loops on the hook (this leaves one loop on the hook). One stitch decreased.

Tip When starting and finishing your tea cosy ensure you have long yarn tails that you can use to seam both sides of the cosy together.

INSTRUCTIONS

TEA-COSY SIDES (MAKE 2)

Row 1: Using 4mm hook and A, ch 29 sts.

Row 2: 1 htr in 3rd ch from hook, htr in each ch to end, turn (27 sts).

Row 3: Ch 2, 13 htr, 2 htr in next st, 13 htr, turn (28 sts).

Row 4: Ch 2, 28 htr, turn.

Row 5: Ch 2, 1 htr in st at the base of the ch, 12 htr, 2 htr in next st, 13 htr, 2 htr in the top of the turning ch, turn (31 sts).

Rows 6–14: Ch 2, 31 htr, turn.

Row 15: Ch 2, miss 1 htr, 13 htr, htr2tog, 13 htr, miss 1 htr, 1 htr into top of the turning ch, turn (28 sts).

Row 16: Ch 2, 28 htr, turn.

Row 17: Ch 2, 13 htr, htr2tog, 13 htr, turn (27 sts).

Row 18: Ch 2, 27 htr, turn.

Row 19: Ch 2, miss 1 htr, 24 htr, miss 1 htr, 1 htr into top of the turning ch, turn (25 sts).

Row 20: Ch 2, miss 1 htr, 22 htr, miss 1 htr, 1 htr into top of the turning ch, turn (23 sts).

Row 21: Ch 2, miss 1 htr, 10 htr, htr2tog, 8 htr, miss 1 htr, 1 htr into top of the turning ch, turn (20 sts).

Row 22: Ch 2, miss 1 htr, 17 htr, miss 1 htr, 1 htr into top of the turning ch, turn (18 sts).

Row 23: Ch 2, miss 1 htr, 7 htr, htr2tog, 6 htr, miss 1 htr, 1 htr into top of the turning ch, turn (15 sts).

Row 24: Ch 2, miss 1 htr, 12 htr, miss 1 htr, 1 htr into top of the turning ch, turn (13 sts). Fasten off and weave in ends.

BUTTONHOLE

Using 4mm hook and A, rejoin yarn to the edge of the left side of the raspberry where the cosy opens for the handle, 5 ch, miss 2 sts, sl st into next st, turn, work 7 dc into ch loop, sl st at base of chain. Fasten off and weave in ends.

CROCHETED CORD

Row 1: With 4mm hook and B, ch 45 sts.

Row 2: Sl st in 2nd ch from hook, sl st in each ch to end (44 sts).

Fasten off and weave in ends. (See page 28.)

FINISHING

Join seams using either slip stitch (see page 23) or whip stitch (see page 35), leaving spaces for the spout and the handle opening. Sew a button on the right-hand side of the cosy to correspond to the buttonhole.

Make three loops in the crocheted cord and secure it firmly to the top of the tea cosy using a tapestry needle. Then secure a button in the centre of the loops.

Technique four

WORKING IN THE ROUND

BY WORKING IN THE ROUND YOU CAN CREATE BOTH FLAT CIRCULAR PROJECTS, SUCH AS COASTERS, AND TUBULAR ONES, SUCH AS BOLSTER CUSHIONS. THESE SHAPES DON'T NEED ANY SEAMS AND WHEN YOU CHANGE COLOURS YOU CAN CREATE AN EVEN STRIPE.

Crocheting in the round is useful for all sorts of projects from placemats to draught excluders. When you become more experienced you could use chunky yarn or scraps of material to make rugs and baskets that are both attractive and durable. Once you have conquered working in the round, then you can tackle a number of popular crochet styles including the granny square (see page 84) or pretty flower motifs.

CREATING A FLAT CIRCLE

Unlike working in rows, to and fro, flat circular pieces are worked with the same side facing you; you don't usually turn the work over. There is also a definite right side and wrong side.

You start by joining the foundation chain into a ring, and then work from the centre outwards. The example below is worked in double crochet.

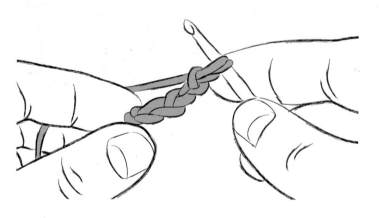

1 Work the number of chain stitches specified in the pattern you are following.

2 Insert the hook into the first chain stitch you made.

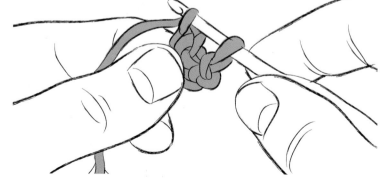

3 Wrap the yarn over the hook and pull through the two stitches on the hook to join the ring. Your first round uses this ring as its foundation.

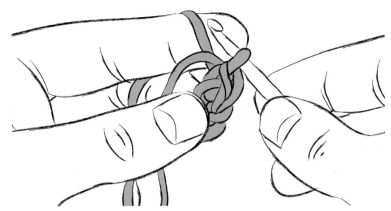

4 Insert your hook into the centre of the ring, yarn over hook. Pull the loop through the centre of the ring (two loops on hook, as in illustration). Yarn over hook, and pull the loop through the two loops on the hook to complete a double-crochet stitch (one loop left on hook).

5 Once you have created the required number of stitches for this first round, you will then join the last stitch made with the first stitch using a slip stitch. The first round is complete.

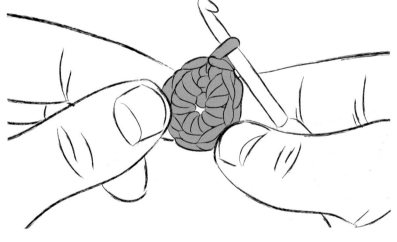

6 At this point you will need to create the height required for the next round. You start by making a chain the equivalent height of the stitch you are working in (see page 22). You can then work your next round.

CREATING A TUBE

The example below is worked in treble crochet.

1 To create a tube, first work the number of chain stitches specified in the instructions for your foundation chain.

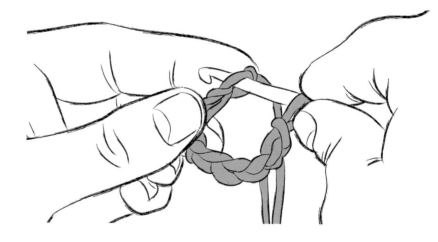

2 Join the last chain to the first chain using a slip stitch.

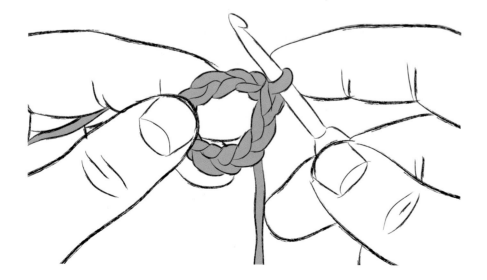

3 Make sure your chain is not twisted.

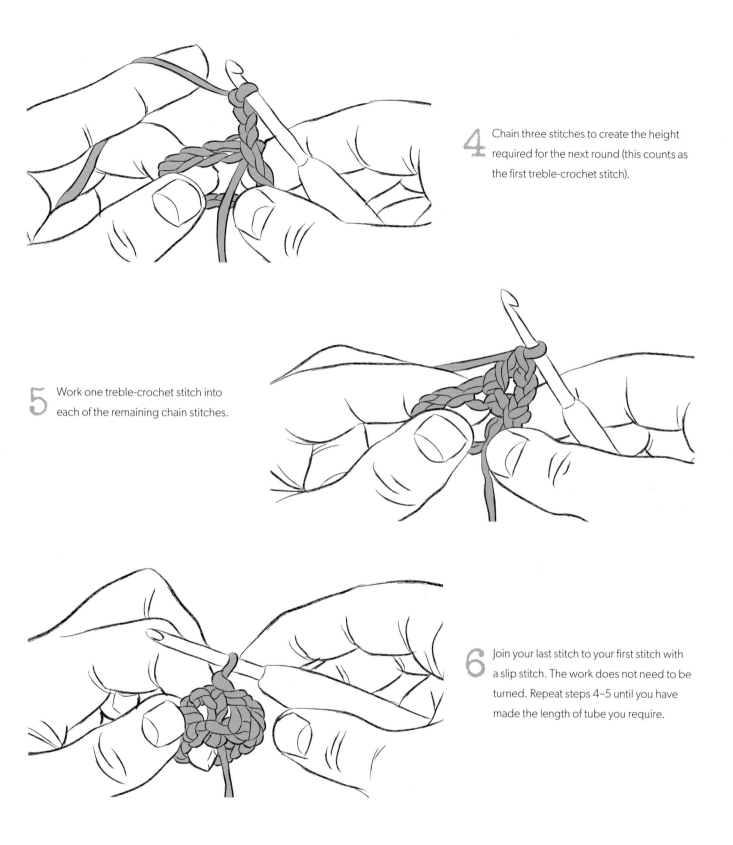

4 Chain three stitches to create the height required for the next round (this counts as the first treble-crochet stitch).

5 Work one treble-crochet stitch into each of the remaining chain stitches.

6 Join your last stitch to your first stitch with a slip stitch. The work does not need to be turned. Repeat steps 4–5 until you have made the length of tube you require.

Tip Place an interlocking stitch marker in the first stitch of a new round to help you keep track of where you are up to (see page 64).

Project four

STRIPY POT HOLDER

THIS POT HOLDER IS A FABULOUS BEGINNERS' PROJECT TO HELP YOU LEARN HOW TO WORK IN THE ROUND AND IS QUICK TO MAKE. THIS VERSION HAS ONE STRIPY SIDE AND ONE PLAIN SIDE. MATCHED TO A FRIEND'S KITCHEN COLOUR SCHEME, IT WOULD MAKE A THOUGHTFUL GIFT.

YOU WILL NEED

• Rowan All Seasons Cotton, 60% cotton, 40% acrylic (98yd/90m per 50g ball):
  1 x 50g ball in 252 Atlas (A)
  1 x 50g ball in 191 Jersey (B)
  1 x 50g ball in 235 Tornado (C)
• 3.5mm (UK9:USE/4) crochet hook
• Tapestry needle

TENSION

Tension is not critical for this project.

FINISHED SIZE

7in (17.5cm) in diameter

TECHNIQUES USED

Treble crochet (tr) (see page 44)
Increasing (see page 51)
Changing colours (see page 27)

INSTRUCTIONS

SIDE 1

Base ring: With 3.5mm hook and A, make 4 ch, join with a sl st to first ch to form a ring.

Round 1: 3 ch (counts as first tr) 11 tr into ring, sl st to top of 3 ch (counts as 12 tr).

Round 2: Change to B, 3 ch, 1 tr into same st, 2 tr into each st to end of round, join with sl st to top of 3 ch (24 sts).

Round 3: Change to C, 3 ch, 1 tr into same st, (1 tr, work 2 tr into next st) 11 times, 1 tr in last st, join with sl st to top of 3 ch (36 sts).

Round 4: Change to A, 3 ch, 1 tr into same st, (2 tr, work 2 tr into next st) 11 times, 2 tr, join with sl st to top of 3 ch (48 sts).

Round 5: Change to B, 3 ch, 1 tr into same st (3 tr, work 2 tr into next st) 11 times, 3 tr, join with sl st to top of 3 ch (60 sts).

Round 6: Change to C, 3 ch, 1 tr into same st, (4 tr, work 2 tr into next st) 11 times, 4 tr, join with sl st to top of 3 ch (72 sts).

Round 7: Change to A, 3 ch, 1 tr into same st, (5 tr, work 2 tr into next st) 11 times, 5 tr, join with sl st to top of 3 ch (84 sts). Fasten off and weave in ends.

SIDE 2

Rep side 1 using just yarn B.

FINISHING

With wrong sides together and working through both layers, join yarn C, 3 ch, 2 tr in st at base of ch, (miss 1 st, 1 dc in next st, miss 1 st, 3 tr in next st), rep around until last 3 sts, miss 1 st, 1 dc in next st, miss 1 st, join with sl st to top of 3 ch.
Fasten off and weave in ends.
To make loop, join yarn C to an edge st on side 2, 12 ch, miss 6 sts, sl st in next st.
Fasten off and weave in ends.

WORKING IN SPIRALS

WORKING IN A SEAMLESS SPIRAL IS PERFECT FOR TOY MAKING AS IT PRODUCES A FABRIC THAT IS ROBUST AND DURABLE ENOUGH TO STAND UP TO ENTHUSIASTIC PLAYMATES. ONCE YOU HAVE MASTERED THIS TECHNIQUE, A WORLD OF EXCITING PATTERNS WILL BE AVAILABLE TO YOU.

Crochet's recent resurgence has been helped by the popularity of Japanese amigurumi – the art of making small stuffed animals and characters. These are made in spirals, so you do not finish each round with a joining slip stitch but instead work continuously round and round.

The most effective stitch to work in spirals is double crochet, as the stitches are short enough to create a smooth spiral. Working in a spiral also means that there is no line created by the turning chain. This type of work is often started with a 'magic circle' (also known as a magic ring; see page 24) that can be pulled up tight so there is no hole or gap left in the centre. Be warned though: making amigurumi can be quite addictive!

USING STITCH MARKERS

After making many mistakes, I now always use a stitch marker when working in crochet spirals. It helps me to identify where each round begins, and is invaluable if you are increasing or decreasing to create shape. Unwanted added stitches can really affect the look of your finished crochet article and using a stitch marker will help you keep track of where you are in the pattern.

You can use an interlocking stitch marker (as shown here), but if you don't have one to hand you could simply use a piece of yarn in a contrasting colour or a safety pin. Place the marker, then when you get to the end of the round, remove the marker, work the stitch and then replace the marker between the last stitch of the previous round and the first stitch of the next round.

WORKING IN A SPIRAL

To work in a spiral you begin by making a magic circle and then build your fabric on that.

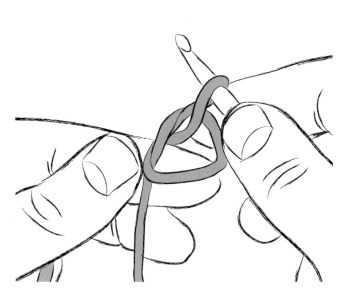

1 Make a basic slip knot. Pull up the loop and slip this loop onto your crochet hook.

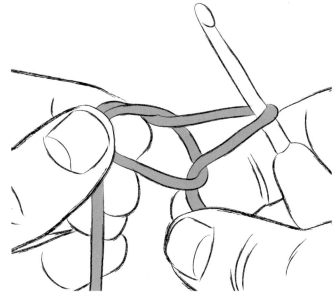

2 Before you tighten the ring, yarn over hook (outside the circle) to make the first chain.

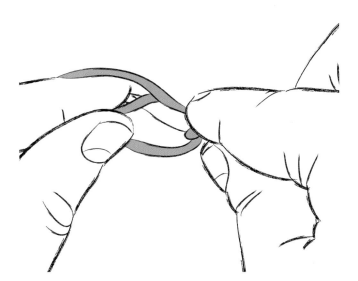

3 Insert the hook into the ring, yarn over hook and pull through the ring so there are two loops on the hook.

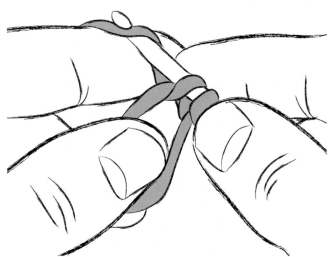

4 Yarn over hook again (outside the circle).

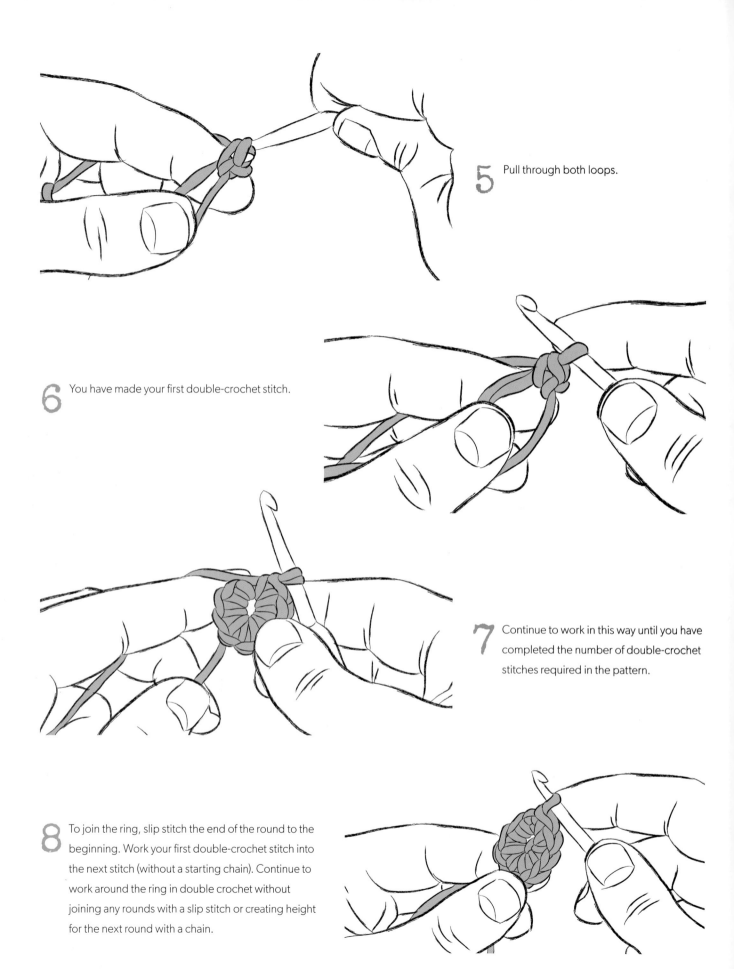

5 Pull through both loops.

6 You have made your first double-crochet stitch.

7 Continue to work in this way until you have completed the number of double-crochet stitches required in the pattern.

8 To join the ring, slip stitch the end of the round to the beginning. Work your first double-crochet stitch into the next stitch (without a starting chain). Continue to work around the ring in double crochet without joining any rounds with a slip stitch or creating height for the next round with a chain.

COUNTING ROUNDS

As you work in rounds you will be able to see that each round of stitches creates a ridge. You can count the ridges to see where you are in the pattern.

You work out from the centre; the first round is the circular centre, and the rounds then grow out from this central point.

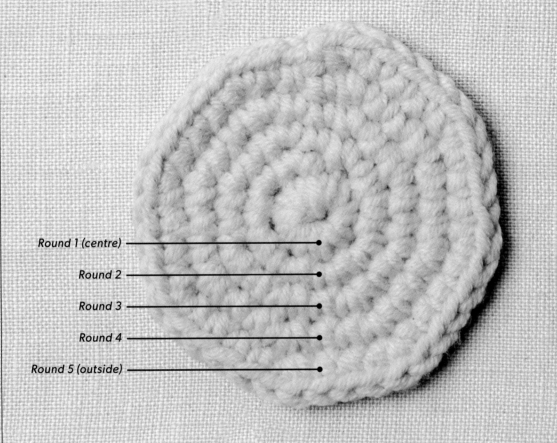

Round 1 (centre)

Round 2

Round 3

Round 4

Round 5 (outside)

BUNNY TOY

THIS SIMPLE BUNNY TOY USES THE AMIGURUMI STYLE OF CROCHET, WORKED IN SPIRALS IN DENSE DOUBLE-CROCHET STITCH. THE PLASTIC SAFETY EYES ARE GREAT FOR MAKING TOYS SAFE TO BE PLAYED WITH, BUT YOU COULD EMBROIDER THE FEATURES IF YOU PREFER.

YOU WILL NEED

- Rico Essentials Alpaca DK, 50% alpaca, 50% wool (136yd/125m per 50g ball): 1 x 50g ball in 02 Beige
- A small amount of cream DK yarn
- 3mm (UK11:US–) crochet hook
- 2 x safety eyes
- Polyester stuffing
- Tapestry needle
- Black embroidery thread
- Embroidery needle

TENSION

6 sts and 6 rows to 1in (2.5cm) over double crochet using 3mm hook.
Use a larger or smaller hook if necessary to obtain the correct tension.

FINISHED SIZE

2¾in (7cm) wide and 5½in (14cm) high

TECHNIQUES USED

Magic circle (MC) (see page 24)
Double crochet (dc) (see page 38)
Increasing and decreasing (see page 50)
Whip stitch (see page 35)
Working into back loop (see page 78)

TECHNIQUE NOTE

On Round 7 you will work through back loop of the stitch. Rather than inserting your crochet hook under both strands of yarn of the stitch you are about to work into, insert your crochet hook under the back loop only (blo). You will see that this forms a ridge in the crocheted fabric (see page 78). On this piece, it demarcates the base of the toy from the body.

Tip When you are making toys for children, you should either use safety eyes or embroider the features with embroidery thread, which won't cause a choking hazard.

INSTRUCTIONS
BODY

Round 1: Using 3mm hook, MC, work 8 dc (8 sts).

Round 2: 2 dc into each st (16 sts).

Round 3: (1 dc, work 2 dc into next st), rep around (24 sts).

Round 4: (2 dc, work 2 dc into next st), rep around (32 sts).

Round 5: (3 dc, work 2 dc into next st), rep around (40 sts).

Round 6: (4 dc, work 2 dc into next st), rep around (48 sts).

Round 7: 1 dc blo around (48 sts).

Round 8: (11 dc, work 2 dc into next st), rep 3 times (52 sts).

Rounds 9–10: Dc around (52 sts).

Round 11: (11 dc, dc2tog), rep 3 times (48 sts).

Rounds 12–26: Dc around (48 sts). At this point, place the eyes on the bunny if you are using safety eyes, then stuff the toy three-quarters full.

Round 27: (4 dc, dc2tog), rep around (40 sts).

Round 28: (3 dc, dc2tog), rep around (32 sts).

Round 29: (2 dc, dc2tog), rep around (24 sts).

Round 30: (1 dc, dc2tog) rep around (16 sts).
Now stuff the rest of the body so that the toy is firm and well-rounded.

Round 31: (dc2tog), rep around (8 sts).
Using a tapestry needle, gather the last 8 sts together and pull closed. Fasten off and weave in ends.

EARS (MAKE 2)

Round 1: Using 3mm hook, MC, work 4 dc (4 sts).

Round 2: 2 dc into each st (8 sts).

Round 3: (3 dc, work 2 dc into next st), rep around (10 sts).

Round 4: (4 dc, work 2 dc into next st), rep around (12 sts).

Round 5: (5 dc, work 2 dc into next st), rep around (14 sts).

Rounds 6–14: Dc around (14 sts).
Fasten off and leave a long tail of yarn.

FINISHING

Using black embroidery thread, sew a small cross onto the front of the bunny for the mouth. On each ear, make a small tuck so the front of the ear is pleated together. Sew the ears firmly onto the head using whip stitch. Make a 1½in (4cm) pompom for the tail using cream yarn. Sew the tail firmly to the back of the bunny.

Tip To make a pompom, cut out two cardboard circles a little smaller than the pompom you want and cut large holes in the centres. Put the rings together and wind lengths of yarn around them, through the middle, until the centre hole is filled. Cut through all the strands of yarn at the outer edge, then ease a length of yarn between the cardboard rings. Tie very firmly around the centre, leaving a tail for sewing. Ease the card discs away, fluff out the strands and trim.

FABRIC PATTERNS

ONCE YOU HAVE THE LEARNT THE BASIC STITCHES, YOU CAN COMBINE THEM TO MAKE A RANGE OF BEAUTIFUL PATTERNS. YOU WILL NOTICE THAT IN MOST CROCHET PATTERNS THE INSTRUCTIONS ARE REALLY JUST ABOUT CHANGING HOW TREBLE, DOUBLE AND CHAIN STITCHES ARE WORKED.

It is fascinating to see the different variations that can be made by simply changing a few instructions. It is worth thinking about the type of fabric you want to make before you choose a pattern. For instance, if you are making an object for the home, such as a tablemat, a pot holder or perhaps a bag, you will want to choose quite a dense, close-weave stitch. Patterns like this are durable and keep their shape because they are unlikely to stretch. If you choose to make this kind of pattern, use a DK-weight wool or cotton yarn so the stitches show up clearly, rather than a fluffy or hairy yarn such as mohair that will obscure the stitches.

Tip Make sure you know where your next stitch should be placed. All crochet stitches (except your beginning chain) will need to be made into existing work. There are lots of different places where you can make your next stitch: into a chain space, between the stitches, or into the front or back loop only. Each will create a different effect. It is worth reading your pattern first to make sure what you will be doing.

Wavy lines (see page 75)

LITTLE LEAF STITCH

This is a pretty, but quite dense stitch, which is suitable for items that will take some wear and tear such as bags, cushions or pencil cases.

Row 1: Work chain stitches for your foundation chain in a multiple of 2 stitches plus 1 stitch.

Row 2: 1 dc in 3rd ch from hook, 1 ch, 1 dc into same st, miss 1 ch, *1 dc, 1 ch, 1 dc into next st, miss 1 ch, rep from * to last st, 1 dc, 1 ch, 1 dc into last st, turn..

Row 3: Ch 2, *into ch sp of previous row work 1 dc, 1 ch, 1 dc, rep from * to end, turn.

Row 2 forms the pattern and is repeated throughout.

Little leaf stitch

PALM LEAVES

If you want to make a pretty garment then you will want a stitch pattern that has longer stitches, maybe a combination of treble or double treble stitches. You could create a more open pattern featuring spaces created by chain stitches. The overall effect will be light and the fabric will have a soft drape.

Row 1: Work chain stitches for your foundation chain in a multiple of 2 stitches plus 1 stitch.

Row 2: 1 dc in 4th ch from hook, *2 ch, miss next 2 ch, 1 dc into next ch, rep from * to end, turn.

Row 3: Ch 3, 1 tr into first dc, *3 tr into next dc, rep from * to end, 2 tr into the top of turning ch, turn.

Row 4: Ch 3, 1 dc into 2nd tr of the first 3 tr group, *2 ch, 1 dc into 2nd tr of next 3 tr group, rep from * to end, working last dc into top of the turning ch, turn.

Rows 3 and 4 form the pattern and are repeated throughout.

palm leaves

WAVY LINES AND ZIGZAGS

By increasing and decreasing crochet stitches at regular intervals you can create wavy lines (see photograph on page 72), undulating ripples or pronounced zigzags. The cowl pattern in this chapter (see page 76) uses a wavy stitch pattern. This brilliant effect is achieved just by increasing and decreasing treble stitches at regular intervals along each row.

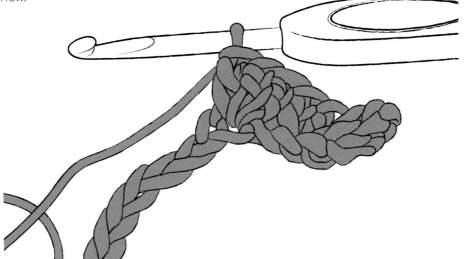

INCREASE

As you increase, you create a group of stitches, or a shell, by working several complete stitches into the same place.

DECREASE

As you decrease, you create a cluster. A number of stitches may be joined into a cluster by gathering together the last loop of several stitches with one last loop. This creates the valleys in wavy lines.

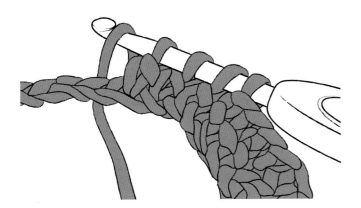

1 Work a treble stitch into each of the next three stitches, leaving the last loop of each on the hook.

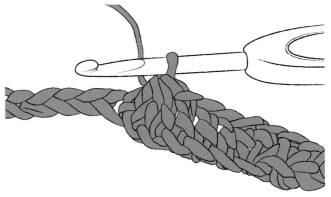

2 Yarn over hook and draw through all four loops on the hook.

WAVY PATTERN COWL

IN WINTER, NOTHING BEATS THE COSY COMFORT OF A COWL. IT LOOKS CHIC AND THE WAY IT DRAPES AROUND THE NECK MEANS THAT YOU CAN ALMOST FORGET YOU ARE WEARING IT. BY THE END OF THE COLD SEASON, THIS COWL WILL HAVE BECOME A MUCH-LOVED OLD FRIEND.

YOU WILL NEED

- Erika Knight Medium British Blue Wool, 100% wool (60yd/55m per 25g ball): 5 x 25g balls in 42 pretty
- 4mm (UK8:USG/6) crochet hook
- Tapestry needle

TENSION

23 sts and 8 rows to 4in (10cm) over wavy stitch pattern using 4mm hook. Use a larger or smaller hook if necessary to obtain the correct tension.

FINISHED SIZE

8¾in (22cm) wide and 28in (71cm) long (before joining)

TECHNIQUES USED

Treble crochet (tr) (see page 44)
Increasing and decreasing (see page 75)

INSTRUCTIONS

COWL

Row 1: Using 4mm hook, ch 43 sts.
Row 2: 1 tr in 3rd ch from hook, *1 tr into each of next 3 ch, over next 3 ch work tr3tog, 1 tr into each of next 3 ch, 3 tr into next ch; rep from * ending last rep with 2 tr in last ch, turn.
Row 3: Ch 3, 1 tr into st at base of ch, *1 tr into each of next 3 tr, over next 3 tr work tr3tog, 1 tr into each of next 3 tr, 3 tr into next tr; rep from *, ending last rep with 2 tr into top of turning ch, turn.
Row 3 forms the pattern. Rep pattern until work measures 28in (71cm).
Do not fasten off.

FINISHING

Sew the first row and the last row together. Fasten off and weave in ends. This cowl also looks great if, before you join the ends together, you twist the strip once.

Tip This cowl is worked in one colour, but it also looks fabulous if you use different colours for alternate rows to give a cheerful wavy stripy pattern.

TEXTURED STITCHES

THERE ARE MANY GREAT WAYS TO CREATE TEXTURE AND PATTERNS IN CROCHET. SOME ARE PURELY DECORATIVE BUT OTHERS CAN HAVE A USEFUL DIMENSION, SUCH AS BACK LOOP ONLY, WHICH PRODUCES THE EQUIVALENT OF RIB STITCH IN KNITTING AND IS USEFUL FOR STRETCHY HEMS.

BACK LOOP ONLY (BLO)

When I first started to crochet I was frustrated that there seemed to be no equivalent to the stretchy rib stitch used in knitting for cuffs and sweater hems. However, I soon discovered the crochet equivalent. Crochet rib stitch is less elastic than its knitting cousin, but it can be used to great effect to edge garments and to create texture. One significant difference with a crochet rib is that it is worked horizontally. It uses the clever trick of working into the back loop only of each stitch on the previous round.

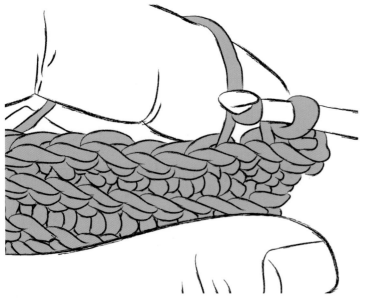

1 Work each stitch only into the back loop of your previous round.

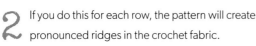

2 If you do this for each row, the pattern will create pronounced ridges in the crochet fabric.

Back loop only
(see page 78)

Puff stitches
(see page 80)

Shell stitches
(see page 81)

PUFF STITCHES

There are many great ways to create texture and interesting patterns in crochet. One easy way is to insert a puff stitch or a bobble stitch into the pattern. Such stitches are made by working several stitches into one stitch. All of those stitches are then gathered at the top as you would with a cluster. As with a cluster stitch (see page 75), each stitch is partially made and then the yarn is pulled through all the loops on the hook to close the stitch together.

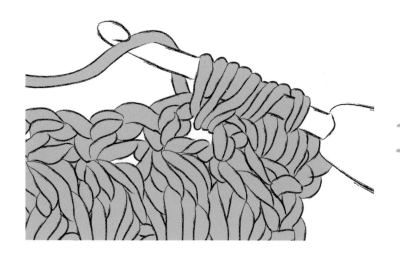

1 Puff stitches bring together a number of half treble stitches. You do this by working a number of partially made stitches as follows. *Yarn over hook, insert hook into ch or st, pull yarn through work, rep from * twice (7 stitches on hook).

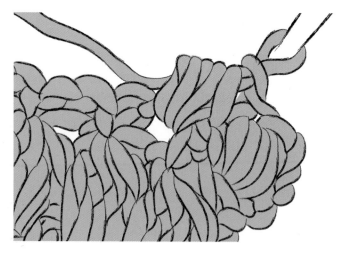

2 Yarn over hook and pull through all 7 loops on hook.

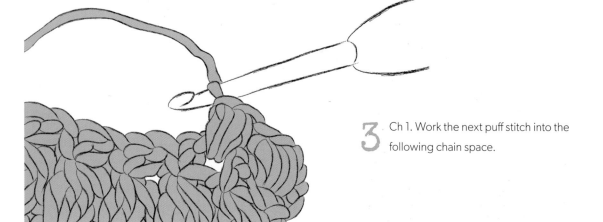

3 Ch 1. Work the next puff stitch into the following chain space.

SHELL STITCHES

As a fan of both knitting and crochet I tend to alternate between the two. One reason I am so glad I learned to crochet is that I now have many different options for creating decorative edges. I often finish off a knitted garment with a crochet edge. By far my favourite edging is the shell pattern. Doris Chan, one of the world's experts on crochet, described shell patterns as the 'showgirl' of the crochet world. I completely agree. It is a simple technique that makes your work look extra-special. A shell is made by working several stitches into a single stitch. In order to keep the rest of your work flat, you need to miss one or more base stitches in the row below.

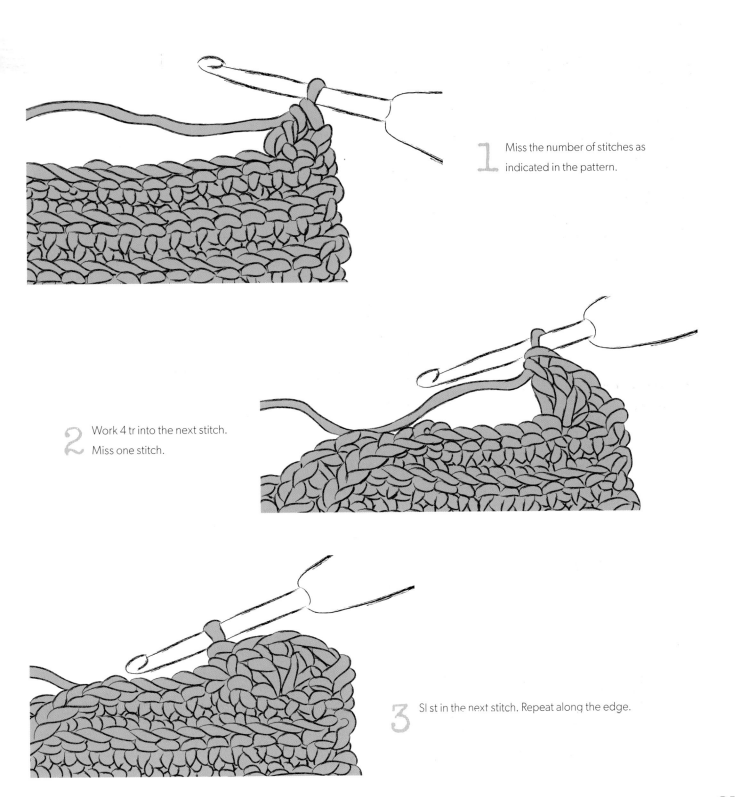

1 Miss the number of stitches as indicated in the pattern.

2 Work 4 tr into the next stitch. Miss one stitch.

3 Sl st in the next stitch. Repeat along the edge.

FINGERLESS MITTENS

FINGERLESS MITTENS HAVE BECOME MORE POPULAR AS WE SPEND MORE TIME TEXTING AND ON COMPUTERS. THEY ARE ALSO HANDY TO WEAR ON COLD WINTER EVENINGS TO CROCHET! THIS PATTERN USES THE RIB TECHNIQUE FOR ELASTICITY, WHILE A PRETTY SHELL PATTERN ADDS DETAIL.

YOU WILL NEED

- King Cole Merino Blend Aran, 100% wool (88yd/80m per 50g ball): 2 x 50g balls in 904 Stone
- 4mm (UK8:USG/6) crochet hook
- 6 x ½in (1.25cm) buttons
- Tapestry needle

TENSION

20 sts and 12 rows to 4in (10cm) over half treble rib using 4mm hook. Use a larger or smaller hook·if necessary to obtain the correct tension.

FINISHED SIZE

4¼in (11cm) wide and 6½in (16.5cm) long

TECHNIQUES USED

Slip stitch (sl st) (see page 23)
Half treble crochet (htr) (see page 47)
Treble crochet (tr) (see page 44)
Working into the back loop only (blo) (see page 78)
Shell stitch (see page 81)

INSTRUCTIONS

RIGHT MITTEN

Row 1: Using 4mm hook, ch 32 sts.
Row 2 (WS): 1 htr in 3rd ch from hook, htr into each ch to end, turn (30 sts).
Row 3: Ch 2, htr blo into each st to end, turn (30 sts).
Row 3 forms the pattern. Work 14 rows.
Row 18: Ch 2, 6 htr blo, 6 ch, miss 6 sts, sl st into next st, htr blo into same st, then each st to end, turn (30 sts).
Row 19: Ch 2, 18 htr blo, htr into each ch of thumbhole, htr blo into each st to end, turn (30 sts).
Work a further 10 rows in pattern.
Next row (buttonhole row and shell pattern): Ch 1, *miss 1 st, 4 tr in next st, miss 1 st, sl st in next st; rep from * 5 times, **4 ch, miss 1 st, sl st in next st; rep from ** twice. Fasten off and weave in ends.

LEFT MITTEN

Row 1: Using 4mm hook, ch 32 sts.
Row 2 (WS): 1 htr in 3rd ch from hook, htr into each ch to end, turn (30 sts).

Row 3: Ch 2, htr blo into each st to end, turn (30 sts).
Row 3 forms the pattern. Work a further 14 rows.
Row 18: Ch 2, 18 htr blo, 6 ch, miss 6 sts, sl st into next st, htr blo into same st, then each st to end, turn (30 sts).
Row 19: Ch 2, 6 htr blo, htr into each ch of thumbhole, htr blo into each st to end, turn (30 sts).
Work a further 10 rows in pattern.
Next row (buttonhole row and shell pattern): *Ch 4, miss 1 st, sl st in next st; rep from * twice, **miss 1 st, 4 tr in next st, miss 1 st, sl st in next st; rep from ** 5 times. Fasten off and weave in ends.

FINISHING

Lay each mitten widthways with WS facing. Fold the shell edge on top of the starting edge, overlapping by two rows. Sew both edges together through the base of the shell pattern. Sew three buttons onto each mitten opposite the buttonholes.

GRANNY SQUARES

THE GRANNY SQUARE IS A CLASSIC CROCHET TECHNIQUE THAT IS WELL WORTH ADDING TO YOUR REPERTOIRE. IT IS PERFECT FOR USING UP ODDMENTS OF YARN AND BUILDING GRADUALLY INTO SOMETHING SPECIAL, BE IT A CUSHION, A THROW OR A FULL-SIZED BLANKET.

I have been a knitter since childhood, but I taught myself to crochet a few years ago because I had an enormous stash of unused yarn that I wanted to put to good use. The great thing about granny squares is that each round uses up small quantities of yarn and you can slowly whittle away at all your odds and ends.

Many people have a granny-square creation in their project bag over a long period of time. They add squares month by month as they use up oddments of yarn. My advice is not to get too hung up on the colour combinations – just reach for your nearest ball of yarn and get going.

Tip When creating a granny square you need to work into a chain space made in the previous row (ch sp), instead of working into a stitch. When you begin a round with a new colour, join it with a slip stitch working into a chain space.

MAKING GRANNY SQUARES

Granny squares are always worked from the centre outwards.

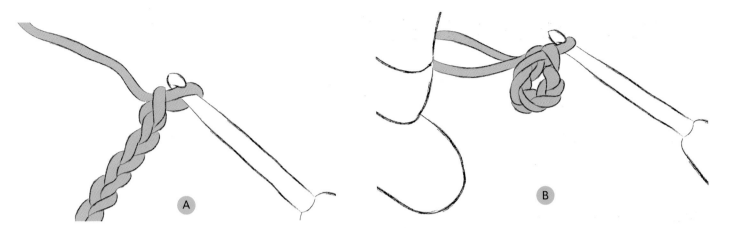

A

B

1 **Round 1:** Using 4mm (UK8:USG/6) hook and first colour, ch 6 sts (**A**). Join with a sl st to form a ring (**B**).

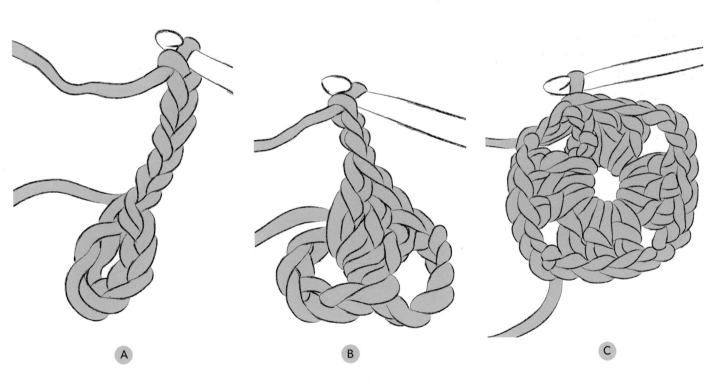

A

B

C

2 **Round 2:** Ch 6 (this counts as the first tr and 3 ch) (**A**), (3 tr into ring (**B**), 3 ch) rep 3 times, 2 tr into ring, sl st into 3rd of 6 ch at the beg of round (**C**). Fasten off.

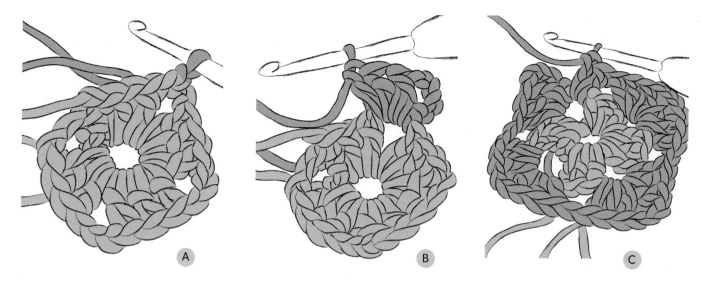

A

B

C

3 Change to second colour. **Round 3:** Attach yarn in any corner chain space using a sl st (**A**), ch 6 (counts as the first tr and 3 ch), 3 tr into same ch sp (**B**), *1 ch, miss 3 tr, (3 tr, 3 ch, 3 tr) into next ch sp, rep from * twice, 1 ch, miss 3 tr, 2 tr into next ch sp (**C**), sl st into 3rd of 6 ch at beg of round. Fasten off.

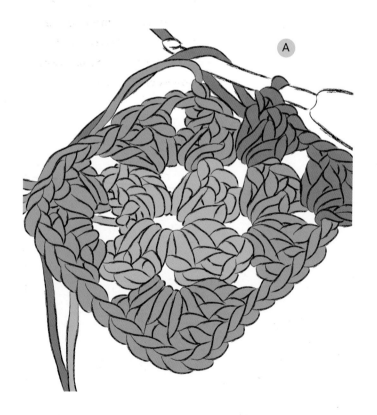

A

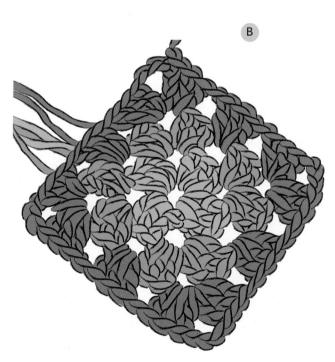

B

4 Change to third colour. **Round 4:** Attach yarn in any corner chain sp using a sl st, ch 6 (counts as the first tr and 3 ch), 3 tr into same ch sp (**A**), *1 ch, miss 3 tr, 3 tr into next ch sp, 1 ch, miss 3 tr, (3 tr, 3 ch, 3 tr) into next ch sp, rep from * twice, 1 ch, miss 3 tr, 3 tr into next ch sp, 1 ch, miss 3 tr, 2 tr into next ch sp, sl st into 3rd of 6 ch at beg of round (**B**). Fasten off.

5 Change to fourth colour. **Round 5:** Attach yarn in any corner chain sp using a sl st, 6 ch (counts as the first tr and 3 ch), 3 tr into same ch sp, *(1 ch, miss 3 tr, 3 tr into next ch sp) twice, 1 ch, miss 3 tr, (3 tr, 3 ch, 3 tr) into next ch sp, rep from * twice, (1 ch, miss 3 tr, 3 tr into next ch sp) twice, 1 ch, miss 3 tr, 2 tr into next ch sp, sl st into 3rd of 6 ch at beg of round. Fasten off.

You can keep going like this, changing the colours for each round and increasing the number of treble clusters in each row until you have a very big square. Alternatively, you can make a number of small squares and join them together to make cushions, blankets or a scarf. One granny square can also make a very quick and easy drinks coaster.

CHOOSING YOUR COLOUR SCHEME

If you are making a blanket or cushion from scratch and want a more colour co-ordinated look, choose one colour for the background or main colour that will tie the whole scheme together. For the blanket pattern in this book I took inspiration from the colours on a birthday card that I really liked and then matched my yarn to that scheme. When it comes to arranging the squares, I always ensure that each square has a different colour combination to the one next to it.

GRANNY-SQUARE BLANKET

THE GRANNY-SQUARE BLANKET IS A CLASSIC CROCHET DESIGN. VINTAGE VERSIONS CAN FETCH QUITE A LOT OF MONEY, SO WHY NOT MAKE YOUR OWN INSTEAD? THIS BLANKET IS MADE IN SOFT, DURABLE COTTON-BLEND YARN, SO IT IS WASHABLE AND PERFECT FOR A PICNIC BLANKET.

YOU WILL NEED

- King Cole Bamboo Cotton DK, 50% bamboo, 50% cotton (251yd/230m per 100g ball):
  2 x 100g balls in 543 Oyster (A)
  1 x 100g ball in 637 Saffron
  1 x 100g ball in 618 Dusty Pink
  1 x 100g ball in 533 Green
  1 x 100g ball in 520 Blush
  1 x 100g ball in 539 Claret
  1 x 100g ball in 609 Glacier
  1 x 100g ball in 527 Opal
  1 x 100g ball in 529 Plum
  1 x 100g ball in 576 Aqua
  (Pick three different colours for the centre rounds of each square but always use A for the final round.)
- 4mm (UK8:USG/6) crochet hook
- Tapestry needle

TENSION

Tension is not critical for this project, but each square is approximately 4 x 4in (10 x 10cm) using a 4mm hook.

FINISHED SIZE

31in (78cm) square
This blanket is made up of 64 squares, eight across by eight down.

TECHNIQUES USED

Slip stitch (sl st) (see page 23)
Double crochet (dc) (see page 38)
Treble crochet (tr) (see page 44)

INSTRUCTIONS
GRANNY SQUARE

Round 1: Using 4mm hook and first colour, ch 6 sts, join with a sl st to form a ring.

Round 2: Ch 6 (this counts as the first tr and 3 ch), (3 tr into ring, 3 ch) 3 times, 2 tr into ring, sl st into 3rd of 6 ch at the beg of round. Fasten off.
Change to second colour.

Round 3: Attach yarn in any corner chain sp, 6 ch (counts as the first tr and 3 ch), 3 tr into same ch sp, *1 ch, miss 3 tr, (3 tr, 3 ch, 3 tr) into next ch sp; rep from * twice, 1 ch, miss 3 tr, 2 tr into next ch sp, sl st into 3rd of 6 ch at beg of round. Fasten off.
Change to third colour.

Tip In this pattern I joined each square to the next as I worked (instead of making the 64 squares individually and joining them later). Doing this means that you can enjoy seeing your work grow gradually.

Round 4: Attach yarn in any corner chain sp, 6 ch (counts as the first tr and 3 ch), 3 tr into same ch sp, *1 ch, miss 3 tr, 3 tr into next ch sp, 1 ch, miss 3 tr, (3 tr, 3 ch, 3 tr) into next ch sp; rep from * twice, 1 ch, miss 3 tr, 3 tr into next ch sp, 1 ch, miss 3 tr, 2 tr into next ch sp, sl st into 3rd of 6 ch at beg of round. Fasten off.

FIRST SQUARE

Round 5: Attach yarn A in any corner chain sp, 6 ch (counts as the first tr and 3 ch), 3 tr into same ch sp, *(1 ch, miss 3 tr, 3 tr into next ch sp) twice, 1 ch, miss 3 tr, (3 tr, 3 ch, 3 tr) into next ch sp; rep from * twice, (1 ch, miss 3 tr, 3 tr into next ch sp) twice, 1 ch, miss 3 tr, 2 tr into next ch sp, sl st into 3rd of 6 ch at beg of round. Fasten off.

If you want to join the squares together as you make the blanket, use the following instructions. If you want to make the 64 squares individually and sew them all together at the end, complete round 5 above on each square.

SECOND SQUARE

Round 5: Attach yarn A in any corner chain sp, 6 ch (counts as the first tr and 3 ch), 3 tr into same ch sp, *(1 ch, miss 3 tr, 3 tr into next ch sp) twice, 1 ch, miss 3 tr, 3 tr, 1 ch, dc into any 3 ch corner sp of first square, 1 ch, then work 3 tr in second square corner ch sp, (1 ch, dc into next 1 ch sp of first square, 3 tr in next 1 ch sp

of round 4 of the second square) twice, 1 ch, dc into next 1 ch sp of first square, 3 tr in next 3 ch sp of round 4 of the second square, 1 ch, dc into 3 ch corner sp of first square, 1 ch, 3 tr in second square corner ch sp. Finish off second square as normal granny round: (1 ch, miss 3 tr, 3 tr into next ch sp) twice, 1 ch, miss 3 tr, (3 tr, 3 ch, 3 tr) into next ch sp, (1 ch, miss 3 tr, 3 tr into next ch sp) twice, 1 ch, miss 3 tr, 2 tr into next ch sp, sl st into 3rd of 6 ch at beg of round. Fasten off.
Two squares have been joined.
Join the next squares like this until a row of eight squares has been completed.

SECOND ROW ONWARDS

Join the first square of the next row to the bottom of the first square of the previous row.
The second square of the second row can be attached to the blanket along two sides. This will be true of the following rows.

SECOND SQUARE, SECOND ROW

Round 5: Attach yarn A in any corner chain sp, 6 ch (counts as the first tr and 3 ch), 3 tr into same ch sp, *(1 ch, miss 3 tr, 3 tr into next ch sp) twice, 1 ch, miss 3 tr, 3 tr in working square corner ch sp, 1 ch, dc into right-hand 3 ch corner sp of square above, 1 ch, then work 3 tr in working square corner ch sp, (1 ch, dc into next 1 ch sp of square above, 3 tr in next 1 ch sp of round 4 of the working square) twice,

1 ch, dc into next 1 ch sp of square above, 3 tr in next 3 ch sp of round 4 of the working square, 1 ch, dc into 3 ch corner sp of square above, 1 ch, 3 tr in working square corner ch sp, (1 ch, dc into next 1 ch sp of first square, 3 tr in next 1 ch sp of round 4 of the working square) twice, 1 ch, dc into next 1 ch sp of first square, 3 tr in next 3 ch sp of round 4 of the working square, 1 ch, dc into 3 ch corner sp of first square, 1 ch, 3 tr in working square corner ch sp. Finish off working square as normal: (1 ch, miss 3 tr, 3 tr into next ch sp) twice, 1 ch, miss 3 tr, 2 tr into next ch sp, sl st into 3rd of 6 ch at beg of round. Fasten off.

Continue to join squares like this along two sides until you have two rows eight squares long. Work until your blanket is eight squares by eight squares. Using a tapestry needle, weave in all the ends.

EDGING

Round 1: Using A, attach yarn to any stitch on the edge of the blanket with a sl st, 1 ch, 1 dc into each stitch and each ch of 1 ch sp, at the corners work (1 dc, 1 ch, 1 dc), sl st into 1 ch at beg of round. Fasten off.
Round 2: Using one of the other colours, rep edging round 1.
Round 3: Using yarn A, rep edging round 1.
Round 4: Rep edging round 2.
Gently block the whole blanket.

LACE STITCHES

LACE PATTERNS IN CROCHET ARE OFTEN WHERE THE MAGIC CAN HAPPEN. SIMPLY BY USING A VERY FINE YARN AND A SMALL HOOK YOU CAN CREATE A GARMENT THAT LOOKS REALLY COMPLICATED AND DELICATE BUT USES THE EASIEST OF STITCHES AND GROWS QUICKLY.

When you get used to working crochet patterns you will soon experience the versatility of this craft. A tightly worked double-crochet stitch can create a dense, hard-wearing fabric. However, at the other end of the scale, you can create delicate open lace fabrics by making large spaces between the stitches and using fine lace-weight yarns.

The great thing about crochet is that you can take any stitch pattern and create a lace effect either by increasing the number of chain stitches that connect the pattern together, or by using a relatively fine yarn with a larger hook than you would usually use with that weight of yarn. If you are making a garment such as a scarf or shawl that doesn't need to have a specific fit, try experimenting with a stitch pattern. Change the yarn and hook to see if you can find a better texture for the pattern you want. The pattern in this section (see page 96) uses a fine mohair yarn. This creates a very pretty effect. In recent years, yarn companies have included Lurex threads or sequins in some of their lace-weight yarns, which would make a very glamorous shawl.

Tip Chain stitches can be tricky to count, especially if you need to create a large number for a foundation chain. I place a stitch marker or safety pin through the loop of every 20th stitch to help me work out how many chains I have made. With lace stitches, such as the shawl pattern in this chapter (see page 96), you don't need to know how many stitches are on each row; instead, count the number of chain arches or loops you have made.

ARCH LACE STITCH

The simplest form of crocheted lace pattern uses a series
of chains to form arches.

Make a loose chain divisible by 4, plus 2 ch.
Row 1: Dc 1 in second ch from hook, *5 ch, miss 3 ch, 1 dc into
next ch, rep from * to end, working 1 dc in last ch, turn.
Row 2: *Ch 5, 1 dc in first ch loop, rep from * to end, turn.
Row 2 forms the pattern; rep throughout.

Arch lace stitch

PICOT STITCHES

Picots are great little stitches that can be used to create a pretty edge or detail to a crochet pattern. Often in traditional Irish lace patterns, a little picot would be added to a chain arch in a lace pattern to create extra detail or to fill a gap. Usually picots are made from three chain stitches.

Work 2 or 3 dc along the edge.

Work 3 chain stitches.

Insert the hook into the same stitch where the last dc was made, yarn over hook, pull the yarn through the work and the loop on the hook to form a sl st. 1 picot made.

Continue to work regular dc stitches in between each picot.

Picot stitches

BLOCKING YOUR WORK

Due to the open pattern of lace pieces, the shape of your crochet can quickly be distorted. What you had hoped would be a light and airy shawl now looks like an unwanted dishrag. Don't despair! It is more important than ever to block your work. When it comes to blocking lace-weight yarns, I submerge my crochet in a bowl of cool water. Once it has soaked for a few minutes, I drain away the water and then gently squeeze out the excess water (never wring the crochet piece). I then place the work between two bath towels and roll the towels into a sausage shape to remove the last of the water. Finally I lay out the piece on a flat surface, pin it into its final shape and allow it to dry for about 24 hours. The final blocked piece of work will look stunning.

Lacy crochet can look very misshapen (above) unless you soak it and block it (below).

LACY SHAWL

THERE IS NOTHING MORE GLAMOROUS FOR AN EVENING OUTFIT THAN A PRETTY LACY SHAWL. THIS PROJECT IS DECEPTIVELY SIMPLE AND WOULD MAKE A BEAUTIFUL GIFT, PERHAPS FOR A BRIDE WHO MIGHT APPRECIATE A HANDMADE 'SOMETHING NEW' TO COVER HER SHOULDERS.

YOU WILL NEED

- Rico Design Fashion Romance, 50% acrylic, 30% mohair, 20% wool (273yd/250m per 25g ball): 2 x 25g balls 04 Ice Blue
- 4mm (UK8:USG/6) crochet hook
- Tapestry needle

TENSION

5½ chain loops and 12 rows to 4in (10cm) over chain stitch using 4mm hook. Use a larger or smaller hook if necessary to obtain the correct tension.

FINISHED SIZE

56in (142.5cm) wide and 20½in (52cm) high

TECHNIQUES USED

Slip stitch (sl st) (see page 23)
Double crochet (dc) (see page 38)

INSTRUCTIONS

SHAWL

Row 1: Using 4mm hook, ch 6 sts. Join to create a loop by working 1 dc into the first ch, turn.

Row 2: Ch 6, 1 dc in 1st of 6 ch, 5 ch, 1 dc into the ch loop of the first row, turn (2 ch loops).

Row 3: Ch 6, 1 dc in 1st of 6 ch, (5 ch, 1 dc into the next ch loop of the previous row) twice, turn (3 ch loops).

Row 4: Ch 6, 1 dc in 1st of 6 ch, (5 ch, 1 dc into the next ch loop of the previous row) three times, turn (4 ch loops).

Row 4 forms the pattern. Rep for each row, increasing the number of times the stitches in brackets are worked by one rep for each row. Rep until 69 rows have been worked. Do not break the yarn.

EDGING

Next row: Ch 4, 1 dc in 1st of 4 ch, (4 ch, 1 dc into the next ch loop of the previous row), rep to end of row, do not turn. (This forms the top edge of the shawl.) Without breaking the yarn, work 4 tr in each ch loop along the diagonal side to base point (row 1) and then work 4 tr in each ch loop along the next diagonal side. Join with a sl st to the 2nd ch of turning ch, turn.

Next row: Ch 4, sl st in tr at base of ch, *1 dc in each of next 3 tr, 4 ch, sl st in tr at base of ch; rep from * along diagonal edges until you reach top edge of shawl. Fasten off and weave in ends.

FINISHING

Block the shawl by pinning it out into an even triangle and lightly spraying it with water. Leave to dry for 24 hours.

EDGINGS

ADDING A PRETTY EDGE TO AN OLD TABLECLOTH OR PILLOWCASE IS A BRILLIANT WAY OF UPCYCLING AND MAKING SOMETHING UNIQUE. BEING ABLE TO CROCHET MAKES IT EASY TO CUSTOMIZE KNITTED GARMENTS AS WELL AS PIECES OF FABRIC WITH DECORATIVE EDGING.

There are many different types of crochet edging and numerous ways of attaching an edge. You can create a pretty edge or braid in a strip and then sew it onto the fabric afterwards. This technique can be used to decorate towels or to create pretty cottage-style edges for kitchen dressers or bookshelves. Alternatively, you can crochet an edging strip directly onto a piece of fabric, knitting or crochet.

If you are edging a crochet or knitted garment or blanket, it is best to prepare by sewing all the seams and weaving in your ends first. Then the last thing you do to finish your work is to make the edge.

It is a good idea to use the same type of yarn as the main item, but maybe in a different colour. Matching your yarn type will ensure that when you wash your item the yarn will react in the same way and

your work won't become distorted. When attaching an edging to fabric, you may find with very open-weave fabric – a natural linen, for example – that it is possible to punch a thin crochet hook through the cloth and double crochet a foundation row around the edge.

With a denser fabric, the best idea is to sew a foundation for your crochet stitches by using a needle and the yarn you will be using for your crochet. You can do this by sewing round your item in blanket stitch (see opposite).

Tip Begin your crochet away from the sewing join, then you are less likely to see where your work started or finished.

MAKING A BLANKET-STITCH FOUNDATION

If you want to add a crocheted edge to a cotton tablecloth or other close-weave fabric item, you will need to edge the item in blanket stitch first to have something to crochet on to.

1 With your edge away from you, bring your needle out through the very edge of the fabric.

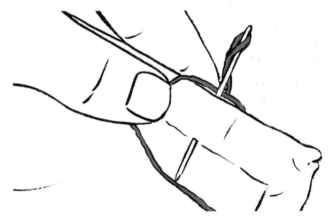

2 Insert your needle to the left and poke into the fabric edge as before, loop the thread around the tip of the needle and pull the needle through.

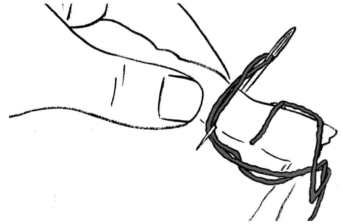

3 Make the next stitch in the same way to the left, making sure the vertical stitches are the same length and the same distance apart. Once you have completed the blanket stitch edge, put the last stitch at the base of where your needle first appeared and then fasten off at the top of the fabric. You will have a line of yarn that sits along the very edge of your fabric. You can now attach your yarn by slipping your crochet hook under this line and beginning with a sl st. I find that I can fit 3 or 4 double crochet stitches in between each vertical blanket stitch.

Tip When you are working around the edge of a blanket or a square napkin, work three stitches into each of the corners so they will be neat and crisp.

DOUBLE CROCHET EDGE OR
CROCHET EDGE FOUNDATION

You can use this to make a neat edge to finish off your work,
or it can act as the first foundation row on which to base more
decorative edge stitches.

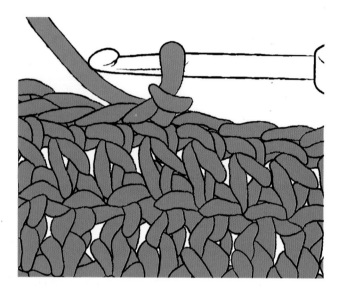

1 Join your chosen yarn to the first stitch on your edge with
a slip stitch, and work 1 ch.

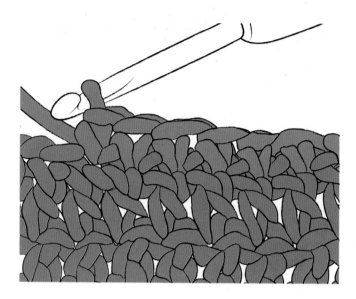

2 Work 1 dc into the first stitch and then into each stitch, space or
hole along the edge of your work, keeping stitches even.

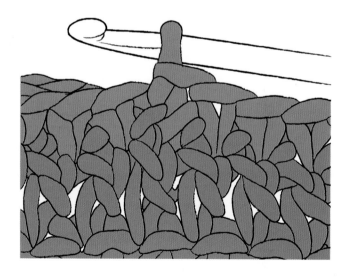

3 Once you have completed your round, join with a sl st into the
first chain.

Tip The first row of crochet edging must be worked
evenly on to a knitted or crocheted piece of work. If the
stitches of the first row are worked unevenly, the finished
edge will spoil the look of the piece.

One row of double crochet gives your work a neat edge (top).
Working two rows of double crochet gives a deeper border
with more impact (above).

TABLECLOTH AND NAPKIN EDGINGS

YOU CAN USE DECORATIVE CROCHET EDGINGS TO TRANSFORM A PLAIN TABLECLOTH AND NAPKINS INTO HEIRLOOMS. THIS PROJECT USES SEWN BLANKET STITCH ROUND THE HEM OF THE EXISTING ITEM AS A BASE ON WHICH TO CROCHET THE DECORATIVE EDGING.

YOU WILL NEED
- Bergère de France Coton Fifty, 50% cotton, 50% acrylic (152yd/140m per 50g ball):
  3 x 50g balls in 23154 Uniforme
- 2mm (UK14:US–) crochet hook
- Tapestry needle
- 4 x napkins
- 1 x 71in (180cm) diameter round tablecloth

TENSION
Tension is not critical for this project.

TECHNIQUES USED
Slip stitch (sl st) (see page 23)
Double crochet (dc) (see page 38)
Blanket stitch (see page 99)

INSTRUCTIONS
NAPKINS
Using a long strand of yarn and a tapestry needle, sew a blanket stitch around the edge of the napkin (see page 99). Make sure each stitch is evenly spaced about ½in (1.25cm) apart.

Row 1: Using 2mm hook, join the yarn to the top of the blanket stitch, 1 ch, work 4 dc into every blanket stitch. At each corner work 4 dc into last blanket stitch of the edge, 1 ch, 4 dc in first blanket stitch of the next edge. Join with sl st in first ch of round.
Row 2: *5 ch, miss 3 dc, sl st in next dc; rep from * to end. Sl st in dc at the base of the first ch.
Fasten off securely and weave in ends.

TABLECLOTH
Using a long strand of yarn and a tapestry needle, sew a blanket stitch around the edge of the tablecloth (see page 99). Make sure each stitch is evenly spaced about ½in (1.25cm) apart.

Row 1: Using 2mm hook and A, join the yarn to the top of the blanket stitch, 1 ch, work 4 dc into blanket stitch. At each corner work 4 dc into last blanket stitch of the edge, 1 ch, 4 dc in first blanket stitch of the next edge. Join with sl st in first ch of round.
Row 2: 4 ch, miss 1 dc, *1 tr in next dc, 1 ch, miss next dc; rep from * around, sl st in 3rd ch of beg 4 ch.
Row 3: *5 ch, miss (1 ch, 1 tr, 1 ch), sl st in the top of next tr; rep from * to end. Sl st in dc at the base of the first ch.
Fasten off securely and weave in ends.

Tip This project would make a wonderful wedding gift with the edgings worked in the couple's favourite colours. You could even embroider the wedding date discreetly on the hem of the wrong side.

Yarn suppliers

The yarns used in these projects should be available from your local yarn or craft store. If you can't find them try some of the websites shown below:

UK

YARNS

Debbie Bliss from Designer Yarns
Units 8–10 Newbridge Industrial Estate
Pitt Street, Keighley
West Yorkshire BD21 4PQ
Tel: +44 (0)1535 664222
www.designeryarns.uk.com

Deramores
Unit 8 Watermark Business Park
Sittingbourne
Kent ME10 5BH
Tel: +44 (0)1795 668144
www.deramores.com

Rowan Yarns
MEZ Crafts UK, 17F Brooke's Mill
Armitage Bridge, Huddersfield
West Yorkshire HD4 7NR
Tel: +44 (0)1484 950630
www.knitrowan.com

Woolyknit
Unit 5 Warth Mill
Huddersfield Road
Diggle, Saddleworth OL3 5PJ
Tel: +44 (0)1457 877984
www.woolyknit.com

GENERAL SUPPLIES

Fred Aldous
37 Lever Street
Manchester M1 1LW
Tel: +44 (0)161 236 4224
www.fredaldous.co.uk

Hobbycraft
E-Commerce Door A
Parkway
Centrum 100 Business Park, Unit 1
Burton Upon Trent DE14 2WA
Tel: +44 (0)330 026 1400
www.hobbycraft.co.uk

John Lewis
Stores nationwide
Tel: +44 (0)1698 545454
www.johnlewis.com

King Cole
Merrie Mills, Snaygill Industrial Estate
Keighley Road, Skipton
North Yorkshire BD23 2QR
Tel: +44 (0)1756 703670
www.kingcole.co.uk

USA

AC Moore
Stores nationwide
Tel: +1-888-226-6673
www.acmoore.com

Hobby Lobby
Stores nationwide
Tel: +1-855-329-7060
www.hobbylobby.com

Michaels
Stores nationwide
Tel: +1-800-642-4235
www.michaels.com

About the author

Emma learnt to knit as a child, and throughout adolescence she was happiest making and creating little projects in her spare time. Throughout her 20s, Emma knitted garments for friends and poor unsuspecting godchildren, but it was only when she had her own son that she started designing. Inspired by the imagination of children, she likes to make garments and toys that bring a smile.

In the past few years Emma has concentrated on crocheted items. She is particularly drawn to the sculptural quality of crochet, and the fact that it can make wonderful intricate patterns and yet be incredibly robust and durable.

Emma has contributed to a number of popular crochet books, and has written *Crocheted Keyrings & Charms* and *Cute Crocheted Animals*, both published by GMC Publications. She has also worked closely with yarn companies and retailers to design exclusive contemporary patterns. She has had a number of successful collaborations with the celebrated knitwear designer Debbie Bliss.

Emma regularly shares her design inspiration and thought processes through her award-winning knitting and crochet blog: emmavarnam.co.uk. 'My blog is about capturing those little moments of creative magic and taking joy in the small things in life,' says Emma.

Inspiration

Books

Cute and Easy Crochet by Nicki Trench (Cico Books, 2011)
Simple Crochet by Sara Sinaguglia (Mitchell Beazley, 2012)

Websites

Browsing on Pinterest, the virtual moodboard site, I can easily lose a few hours! It is great for colour combination ideas.
pinterest.com

The blog of Lucy at Attic 24 is a crochet institution and a must for all those new to the craft. *attic24.typepad.com*

Most days I check out the inspiration blog of New York craft shop Purl Soho. *purlsoho.com*

Acknowledgements

I would like to thank the wonderful team at GMC, particularly Wendy and Gerrie. Thanks must also go to the editor, Nicola Hodgson; photographers, Sarah Cuttle and Rebecca Mothersole; and the illustrators Martin Woodward, Joshua Brent and Alexander Singleton. Thank you also to Jude Roust who did a brilliant job of checking the patterns.

I have some faithful people who have helped me check whether these patterns work – my indispensable friend, Sue Sherry, and the very clever Rachel Cornes. Thank you to all the inspirational women in my life who had faith that I could do more than I ever dreamed: Helen Varnam, Lynn Swart, Cathy Fisher and Heather Smith.

Finally, a big thank you must go to my darlings, Robert and Benjamin. I love you and you bring the biggest smile to my face.

GMC Publications would like to thank: Christian and Rhoda Funnell, for allowing us to photograph at the Old Forge in South Heighton, East Sussex, UK (www.christianfunnell.com) and Amelia Holmwood for styling and modelling.

Index

To order a book, or to request
a catalogue, contact:

GMC Publications Ltd
Castle Place, 166 High Street,
Lewes, East Sussex,
BN7 1XU
United Kingdom
Tel: +44 (0)1273 488005
www.gmcbooks.com